S0-CAP-739

# Priorities of a Faithful Teacher

# Priorities of a Faithful Teacher

by
John MacArthur, Jr.

"GRACE TO YOU"
P.O. Box 4000
Panorama City, CA   91412

©1991 by
JOHN F. MACARTHUR, JR.

All rights reserved. No part of this book may be reproduced in any form without permission in writing from the publisher, except in the case of brief quotations embodied in critical articles or reviews.

All Scripture quotations, unless noted otherwise, are from the *New American Standard Bible,* © 1960, 1962, 1963, 1968, 1971, 1972, 1973, 1975, and 1977 by The Lockman Foundation, and are used by permission.

ISBN: 0-8024-5333-3

1 2 3 4 5 Printing/LC/Year 95 94 93 92 91

*Printed in the United States of America*

# Contents

These Bible studies are taken from messages delivered by Pastor-Teacher John MacArthur, Jr., at Grace Community Church in Sun Valley, California. These messages have been combined into a 7-tape album titled *Priorities of a Faithful Teacher*. You may purchase this series either in an attractive vinyl cassette album or as individual cassettes. To purchase these tapes, request the album *Priorities of a Faithful Teacher*, or ask for the tapes by their individual GC numbers. Please consult the current price list; then send your order, making your check payable to:

"GRACE TO YOU"
P.O. Box 4000
Panorama City, CA 91412

Or call the following toll-free number:
1-800-55-GRACE

# 1

# Marks of the Faithful Preacher—Part 1

## Outline

Introduction
A. The Preacher's Charge
B. The Preacher's Accountability
C. The Preacher's Portrait
D. The Preacher's Faithfulness

Lesson
I. The Seriousness of the Preacher's Commission (v. 1)
A. His Compelling Responsibility (v. 1a)
B. His Coming Evaluation (v. 1b)
   1. The Judge's identity
   2. The Judge's duty
   3. The Judge's presence
   4. The Judge's evaluation
   5. The Judge's coming

Conclusion

## Introduction

### A. The Preacher's Charge

Studying this letter from the apostle Paul to Timothy, his young son in the faith, is like treading on sacred ground, for it's the last words ever penned by Paul in Scripture. We can only imagine what was racing through his heart as he besought Timothy, who was going to take his place, to be faithful in the ministry. That changing of the guard would occur soon, for Paul knew he would soon be martyred (2 Tim. 4:6-9). Paul would pass the baton to a young man who was moral and virtuous, but possibly timid. It seems Timothy didn't have Paul's the strength of character, conviction, or boldness. So at this late point in Paul's life, he was compelled to give a final and solemn charge.

Paul's instruction is not only for Timothy, but also for every preacher. That makes it relevant for each believer because the believer is responsible to hold the preacher accountable to the standard of God's Word. And the preacher should want that kind of accountability because he is to be an example for the church to follow.

B. The Preacher's Accountability

The Bible is not nebulous, but explicit, about what God expects from the preacher. Second Timothy 4:1-5 contains nine commands. Its exhortative style presents demands, not suggestions, ideas, or points of discussion. It's the pattern Timothy and all who follow after him are responsible to fulfill.

The preacher's role is vital, for God has designed that His people be taught by gifted men. Much of the believer's spiritual growth directly relates to the effectiveness of the preaching he or she is under. So it's a serious issue with God for preachers to live by God's standards and for believers to hold them accountable. And it's vital that people respond in obedience to proper preaching.

Today one of the tragedies in our nation and world is the demise of faithful, consistent, uncompromising, biblical preaching. Certainly some of the blame lies at the preachers' feet, but it also lies at the feet of believers who fail to hold the preacher accountable.

C. The Preacher's Portrait

The English preacher John Bunyan wrote *The Pilgrim's Progress*, an allegory about the Christian life. He wrote that story from Bedford Jail, where he was imprisoned for preaching. Bunyan depicted the Christian life through Pilgrim, who was embarking on a spiritual pilgrimage. Pilgrim was first taken to Interpreter's House because there were some things he needed to know to make his pilgrimage successful. Inside Interpreter's House he was shown a portrait of a preacher that he might realize the importance of the preacher's office. The portrait "had eyes lifted up to heaven, the best of books in his hand, the law of truth was written upon his lips, the world was behind his back. [He] stood as if [he] pleaded with men, and a crown of gold did hang over his head" ([New York: Simon and Schuster, 1957], p. 28).

In 2 Timothy 4 the apostle Paul also paints a preacher's portrait. Only his painting was inspired by God, so it's more than instructive—it's binding. And it delineates the preacher's role in unmistakable terms.

D. The Preacher's Faithfulness

Paul wrote his final letter as a prisoner and recognized that his earthly ministry was near completion. He was able to say, "I have fought the good fight, I have finished the course, I have kept the faith" (2 Tim. 4:7). He wanted Timothy to be able to say the same thing, so he exhorted him to be faithful. In doing so, Paul set for us the divine standard by which faithfulness is measured. It's a running theme throughout his letter.

1. 2 Timothy 1:6-7, 13—"I remind you to kindle afresh the gift of God which is in you through the laying on of my hands. For God has not given us a spirit of timidity, but of power and love and discipline. Therefore do not be ashamed of the testimony of our Lord, or of me His prisoner; but join with me in suffering for the gospel. . . . Retain the standard of sound words which you have heard from me."

2. 2 Timothy 2:1-2—"Be strong in the grace that is in Christ Jesus. And the things which you have heard from me in the presence of many witnesses, these entrust to faithful men, who will be able to teach others also."

3. 2 Timothy 2:8, 14—"Remember Jesus Christ. . . . Remind them of these things, and solemnly charge them in the presence of God."

4. 2 Timothy 3:14—"Continue in the things you have learned."

Second Timothy 4:1-5 summarizes Paul's hope for every Christian pastor. Timothy had a difficult task ahead of him where he was ministering. The church in Ephesus had already begun to defect spiritually. When Paul founded the church, it was in the heat of revival. But over the years, sound doctrine lost its primacy, and godliness was no longer a main issue. In addition, a rampant, empire-wide persecution was beginning to foment, which had the potential of costing Timothy his life. Because the ministry ahead of him was not easy, it was imperative for Timothy to be faithful. So in his parting words Paul gave Timothy the marks of a faithful preacher.

### Lesson

## I. THE SERIOUSNESS OF THE PREACHER'S COMMISSION (v. 1)

"I solemnly charge you in the presence of God and of Christ Jesus, who is to judge the living and the dead, and by His appearing and His kingdom."

### A. His Compelling Responsibility (v. 1a)

"I solemnly charge you."

Those words speak of the seriousness of ministry. The Greek term translated "solemnly charge" (*diamarturomai*) means "to earnestly testify." The aged warrior Paul sought to arm his young son in the faith with a keen sense of his weighty responsibility. Such seriousness is characteristic of a godly individual committed to serving Christ. Paul was like the Reformer John Knox, who said, "Give me Scotland or I die!" When compelled to preach, it is well reported that Knox locked himself in a room and wept for days because he feared the seriousness of his calling. Timothy was to take his calling just as seriously.

In discussing the tongue the apostle James said, "Let not many of you become teachers, my brethren, knowing that as such we shall incur a stricter judgment" (James 3:1). The man or woman who doesn't offend with his or her tongue is perfect, but alas, "no one can tame the tongue" (v. 8). Because of that, no man should rush into a preaching or teaching ministry. If he is not specially called or gifted by God, he will easily offend with his tongue and incur a greater judgment. The ministry is a serious place for those who regard its tasks in earnest.

The whole tone of Paul's charge is a forward look to the second coming of Christ. Nothing will develop accountability like the pastor's realization that he is not primarily responsible to a church, denomination, or school but to God.

B. His Coming Evaluation (v. 1b)

"In the presence of God and of Christ Jesus, who is to judge the living and the dead, and by His appearing and His kingdom."

1. The Judge's identity

"Of God *even* of Christ Jesus" (emphasis added) is probably a better translation, meaning that Paul was charging Timothy in the presence of God, who is Christ Jesus. One cannot be dogmatic about that interpretation since the verse could be speaking of a solemn charge made in the presence of both the Father and the Son. But the former seems preferable not only for linguistic reasons but also because of the underlying theology. John 5 clearly reveals that the one who judges the living and dead is Jesus Christ: "Not even the Father judges anyone, but He has given all judgment to the Son. . . . [God] gave Him authority to execute judgment, because He is the Son of Man" (vv. 22, 27).

2. The Judge's duty

In addition to affirming Christ's deity, Paul also affirmed His duty as Judge. "I solemnly charge you in the presence of God and of Christ Jesus" parallels the common format for court subpoenas in ancient days. An ancient court document commonly read something like this: "The case will be drawn up against you in the court at [the name of the city] in the presence of [the name of the judge]." In using legal terminology, Paul was saying a future subpoena will be served for the preacher to appear before God.

3. The Judge's presence

The preacher's ministry occurs in the presence of the Judge. That provides for an unusual court setting. Typically, those subpoenaed for a trial must tell the truth so the judge will have all the facts. But as divine Judge, Christ already knows the truth! It's a compelling thought to realize the one whom you will appear before is aware of every detail in your life. The pastor's ministry is in full view of His watchful eye.

Now this isn't the only time Paul gave Timothy a compelling charge in view of the Lord's presence. In 1 Timothy 5:21 he says, "I solemnly charge you in the presence of God and of Christ Jesus and of His chosen angels, to maintain these principles." In 1 Timothy 6:13-14 he repeats, "I charge you in the presence of God, who gives life to all things, and of Christ Jesus, who testified the good confession before Pontius Pilate, that you keep the commandment without stain or reproach, until the appearing of our Lord Jesus Christ." There's a compelling seriousness in what we do because God, who sees everything, is who we answer to. Not one month, week, day, hour, or minute escapes His vision. He knows what you do with your time, energies, and opportunities.

4. The Judge's evaluation

The Greek term translated "judge" in 1 Timothy 4:1 (*krinō*) speaks of an evaluation, not condemnation. From *krinō* we derive the words "criteria" and "critic." The phrase "who is to judge" carries the idea of "someone who is on the brink of rendering judgment" Paul wanted to paint a picture of imminence for Timothy.

Christ's evaluation will determine the believer's reward, which will determine his or her level of service in heaven. First Corinthians 3 says that works of gold, silver, and precious stones will last, but those of wood, hay, and stubble will be burned up (vv. 12-15). Second Corinthians 5:10 says, "We must all appear before the judgment seat of Christ, that each one may be recompensed for his deeds in the body, according to what he has done, whether good or bad." For the good we did in serving Christ, we will be rewarded. Our reward will be eternally manifested throughout the entire kingdom by our capacity to serve. While our heavenly inheritance refers to the breadth of our authority, our heavenly reward speaks of the nature of our service in eternity.

Paul and the other apostles lived in light of that divine evaluation. Peter said, "[God] ordered us to preach to the people, and solemnly to testify that this is the

12

One who has been appointed by God as Judge of the living and the dead" (Acts 10:42). Paul, in his sermon on Mars Hill, said, "[God] has fixed a day in which He will judge the world in righteousness through [Christ,] whom He has appointed, having furnished proof to all men by raising Him from the dead" (17:31). And in Romans 2:16 Paul tells of a day when "God will judge the secrets of men through Christ Jesus."

First Corinthians 4:1-5 summarizes the believer's future evaluation like this: "Let a man regard us in this manner, as servants of Christ, and stewards of the mysteries of God. In this case, moreover, it is required of stewards that one be found trustworthy. But to me it is a very small thing that I should be examined by you, or by any human court; in fact, I do not even examine myself. For I am conscious of nothing against myself, yet I am not by this acquitted; but the one who examines me is the Lord. Therefore do not go on passing judgment before the time [of Christ's judgment], but wait until the Lord comes who will both bring to light the things hidden in the darkness and disclose the motives of men's hearts; and then each man's praise will come to him from God."

The implication is that the preacher's evaluation comes from God, not man. People try to evaluate a pastor, but they can't know his heart or motives. Even when you don't know anything against the pastor, and even when the pastor doesn't know anything against himself, God may know something. So God's verdict on his ministry might be different from man's. Only when God reads the heart is it certain that the praise is justified. So the preacher must seek to please God alone. In denying the accusation that he was a man-pleaser, Paul said, "Am I now seeking the favor of men, or of God? Or am I striving to please men? If I were still trying to please men, I would not be a bond-servant of Christ" (Gal. 1:10).

First Timothy 4:1 states that Christ will judge "the living and the dead." That broadens the picture beyond believers to include all who have ever lived. The one who will evaluate the pastor's ministry is the very one who judges all people. Neither death nor life allows any person to escape His judgment. The living and the dead are categories into which everyone falls.

## When Will the Judge Judge?

1. **The First Stage**

   When the Lord takes the church out of the world (1 Thess. 4:13-18), there will be an evaluation of believers at what is known as "the judgment seat of Christ" (Gk., *bēma*, 2 Cor. 5:10). Christ will evaluate the good we have done and reward us accordingly. There will be no condemnation here because there is "no condemnation for those who are in Christ Jesus" (Rom. 8:1). The *bēma* is the first point of judgment in the end, and it is for believers only.

2. **The Second Stage**

   The next point of judgment occurs on earth at Christ's second coming. It is the judgment of the sheep and goats (Matt. 25:14-30), which is for both believers and unbelievers. In that judgment Christ will separate the godly from the ungodly. Believers will then enter His kingdom, but the wicked will "go away into eternal punishment" (v. 46).

3. **The Third Stage**

   The final point of judgment occurs in heaven at the end of the millennium. It is the Great White Throne Judgment, which is for unbelievers only. God will bring all the unbelieving dead from all the ages before His throne for final judgment and condemnation to hell. Revelation 20 says, "The sea gave up the dead which were in it, and death and Hades gave up the dead which were in them; and they were judged, every one of them according to their deeds. And death and Hades were thrown into the lake of fire. This is the second death, the lake of fire. And if anyone's name was not found written in the book of life, he was thrown into the lake of fire" (vv. 13-15).

   5. **The Judge's coming**

      Paul based his solemn charge to Timothy not only on Christ's imminent judgment but also on His "appearing" (Gk., *epiphaneia*, 2 Tim. 4:1). That refers to Christ's second coming, when "every eye will see Him" (Rev. 1:7). When that happens, the church will already have been raptured, its rewards already bestowed in the secrecy of heaven. In glorious liberation, God's children will return to reign with Christ, and their rewards for service will be on full display before the whole world.

*Epiphaneia* literally means "to appear upon." That Christ will again appear upon the earth was a strong motivating factor for Paul in ministry. He eagerly anticipated that great event. In 1 Timothy 6:14 he says, "Keep the commandment without stain or reproach until the appearing of our Lord Jesus Christ." Near the end of his life he said, "In the future there is laid up for me the crown of righteousness, which the Lord, the righteous Judge, will award to me on that day; and not only to me, but also to all who have loved His appearing" (2 Tim. 4:8). In Titus 2:13 he says to be "looking for the blessed hope and the appearing of the glory of our great God and Savior, Christ Jesus."

In ancient days the word *epiphaneia* was used in two special ways. One referred to an obvious intervention by some god. But more often it was used in connection with a Roman emperor, particularly when he came to visit a village or town. To prepare for the emperor's coming, the people would sweep the streets and otherwise clean their town. They attempted to have everything in perfect order for his appearing.

It's as if Paul were saying to Timothy, "You know what happens in a town when people are anticipating the emperor's arrival. But you are expecting the *epiphaneia* of Jesus Christ! Therefore, minister in such a way that, when Christ arrives, He will be pleased with what He sees." To the peasant villager, nothing could exceed the thrill of having the emperor see and approve his or her work. Similarly, we as Christians are to look forward to Christ's appearing and desire His divine and eternal approval.

Christ's appearing will lead to the speedy establishment of "His kingdom" (2 Tim. 4:1). He will come as Judge and reign as King. Sinners will be judged, and believers will be rewarded. The godly will be ushered into His millennial kingdom on earth, but the ungodly will be cast into eternal punishment. Until the Lord returns or calls him home, the preacher is to be faithful. That way he'll receive his proper reward as he shares in the glories and joys of the coming kingdom.

# Conclusion

The preacher must realize the seriousness of his task and be consummately dedicated to it. The task is serious because it comes under the scrutiny of the Judge's evaluation. The perfect Judge will render perfect judgment on the nature, dedication, faithfulness, and consistency of the preacher's efforts. Then it will be seen if what he did was in fact gold, silver, and precious stones or wood, hay, and stubble. The world can push the pastor to compromise his ministry by trying to please others. But if he's mindful of the one he answers to, it will help keep him strong.

Timothy needed to understand the seriousness of his commission because he was going to receive much pressure to compromise his ministry. But pleasing God is the right path, for in the day of His appearing, Christ will reward the faithful in a glorious way. So if you teach a biblical message, the pressure's on, but having the perspective that God is Judge will help keep you on track. The teacher must answer to the Lord, and so must all those he teaches.

## Focusing on the Facts

1. Why is 2 Timothy special? What makes it relevant and important for each believer (see pp. 7-8)?
2. What is much of the believer's spiritual growth directly related to (see p. 8)?
3. Why is the apostle Paul's portrait of a preacher binding (see pp. 8-9)?
4. Second Timothy 4:1-5 summarizes Paul's hope for every Christian _____(see pp. 8-9).
5. Why was the ministry ahead of Timothy not easy? Because of that what was it imperative for him to be (see pp. 9-10)?
6. How does James's comment about teachers (3:1) apply to the serious tone of 2 Timothy 4 (see p. 10)?
7. What does Paul's charge in 2 Timothy 4:1 look forward to (see p. 10)?
8. Why was Paul using legal terminology in 2 Timothy 4:1 (see p. 11)?
9. In what way will judgment before Christ be in a very unusual court setting (see pp. 11-12)?
10. What will determine the believer's reward and level of service in heaven (see p. 12)?
11. What did God order the apostle Peter to preach (Acts 10:42; see pp. 12-13)?

12. What does 1 Corinthians 4:1-5 imply about the preacher's evaluation (see p. 13)?
13. Paul said, "If I were still trying to please _____, I would not be a bond-servant of Christ" (Gal. 1:10; see p. 13).
14. Identify the different stages of judgment (see p. 14).
15. What does the term "appearing" in 2 Timothy 4:1 refer to (see p. 14)?
16. How was *epiphaneia* used in ancient days? How does that apply to the believer (see p. 15)?

## Pondering the Principles

1. Since the believer is responsible to hold preachers accountable to the standard of God's Word, it's imperative for him or her to understand their biblical role. Bible teacher Alexander Strauch wrote, "Since the life of the church depends to a large degree upon its leaders, the proper understanding and practice of church leadership through the elders is crucial to everyone's welfare. . . . Therefore, biblical eldership is not a topic to be studied only by scholars or church leaders. Rather, it should be studied by every believer because it directly affects each one—fathers, mothers, children, widows, the poor, the influential, the sick, the old, and even new believers" (*Biblical Eldership* [Littleton, Colo.: Lewis and Roth, 1986], p. xi). Resolve to better understand the preacher's biblical role, realizing it directly affects your spiritual welfare and that of those you love.

2. Believers will one day stand at the judgment seat of Christ "that each one may be recompensed for his deeds in the body, according to what he has done, whether good or bad" (2 Cor. 5:10). In light of that coming evaluation, strive to please God, not people (Gal. 1:10). Look up the following examples to see if the choice was to follow God or man, noting the result of that choice:

   • Exodus 32:1-28

   • Joshua 24:15

   • 1 Samuel 15:1-26

   • 2 Samuel 11:1-17; 12:9-14

   • 1 Kings 18:17-40

- Daniel 3:8-30

- Luke 10:38-42

- Acts 5:17-29

Ask the Lord to help you obey the admonition of Colossians 3:23-24: "Whatever you do, do your work heartily, as for the Lord rather than for men; knowing that from the Lord you will receive the reward of the inheritance. It is the Lord Christ whom you serve."

# 2

# Marks of the Faithful Preacher—Part 2

**Outline**

Introduction

Review
I.   The Seriousness of the Preacher's Commission (v. 1)

Lesson
II.  The Essence of the Preacher's Commission (v. 2a)
A. Timothy's Character
B. Timothy's Message
III. The Scope of the Preacher's Commission (v. 2b-f)
A. He Is Always Ready to Minister (v. 2b)
B. He Exposes Sin (v. 2c)
C. He Encourages Right Behavior (v. 2d)
D. He Is Patient (v. 2e)
E. He Teaches Sound Doctrine (v. 2f)

Conclusion

**Introduction**

In 2 Timothy 4:1-5 Paul summarizes the requirements of a faithful preacher: "I solemnly charge you in the presence of God and of Christ Jesus, who is to judge the living and the dead, and by His appearing and His kingdom: preach the word; be ready in season and out of season; reprove, rebuke, exhort, with great patience and instruction. For the time will come when they will not endure sound doctrine; but wanting to have their ears tickled, they will accumulate for themselves teachers in accordance to their own desires; and will turn away their ears from the truth, and will turn aside to myths. But you, be sober in all

19

things, endure hardship, do the work of an evangelist, fulfill your ministry."

The faithful teacher and preacher will pay attention to whatever undergirds the quality of his spiritual life. Although those qualities may never become public knowledge, they are under the watchful eye of God, who will evaluate all things. Paul ministered in light of that coming evaluation and wanted Timothy, his son in the faith, to do the same. We too are to manifest spiritual excellence before God and others. That comes by adhering to the marks of a faithful teacher.

### Review

I. THE SERIOUSNESS OF THE PREACHER'S COMMISSION (v. 1; see pp. 10-15)

A. His Compelling Responsibility (v. 1a; see pp. 10-11)

B. His Coming Evaluation (v. 1b; see pp. 12-15)

### Lesson

II. THE ESSENCE OF THE PREACHER'S COMMISSION (v. 2a)

"Preach the word."

Although that command is brief, it states the essence of the teacher's task.

### A Father's Wise Advice to His Son

When I was a young boy, I told my father that I believed God had called me to preach. He gave me a Bible and wrote these words inside it: "Dear Johnny, Preach the Word! 2 Timothy 4:2." It was a simple statement, but it became the compelling charge of my heart. Ever since that day, his biblical advice has remained with me.

The Greek verb translated "preach" (*kērussō*) means "to herald" or "proclaim publicly." Back in the days before radio and television an emperor made a public proclamation or announcement through a messenger. In its biblical sense *kērussō* refers to one who publicly proclaims God's Word. In saying he "was appointed a preacher" (1 Tim. 2:7; 2 Tim. 1:11), the apostle Paul identified himself as a public herald of Scripture.

## A. Timothy's Character

Publicly proclaiming God's Word isn't an easy task. Perhaps that was especially true for Timothy. It seems he was timid and lacked Paul's strength and courage. His young age apparently caused some believers to be suspicious of him (1 Tim. 4:12). Furthermore, Timothy might have felt inadequate in proclaiming Scripture for fear he would have to debate sophisticated false teachers and counter their well-developed polemic. Timothy knew that proclaiming God's Word meant facing hostility and persecution. In those days opposition came from both the Jewish people, who as a whole were antagonistic to the gospel, as well as from the Romans, who held Paul prisoner. Although proclaiming God's Word is not an easy task, Timothy was to do what others before him had done:

1. 2 Peter 2:5—Noah was "a preacher of righteousness" in a wicked society.

2. Jonah 3:4—"Jonah . . . cried out and said, 'Yet forty days and Nineveh will be overthrown.' " His message of doom resulted in that great city's repentance (v. 5).

3. Matthew 3:1-2—"John the Baptist came, preaching in the wilderness of Judea, saying, 'Repent, for the kingdom of heaven is at hand.' " The forerunner of Christ boldly proclaimed a message of repentance and lost his life for condemning a king's infidelity (14:1-4).

4. Matthew 4:17—"Jesus began to preach and say, 'Repent, for the kingdom of heaven is at hand.' " Christ, the prince of all preachers, proclaimed a message of repentance.

## B. Timothy's Message

Timothy was to preach "the word" (2 Tim. 4:2): God's Word. This was not the only time Paul mentioned God's Word to Timothy. In the previous chapter he states, "From childhood you have known the sacred writings which are able to give you the wisdom that leads to salvation through faith which is in Christ Jesus. All Scripture is inspired by God and profitable for teaching, for reproof, for correction, for training in righteousness" (3:15-16). Timothy was also told to "retain the standard of sound words" he received from Paul (1:13). Paul also said, "Be diligent to present yourself approved to God as a workman who does not need to be ashamed, handling accurately the word of truth" (2:15).

Timothy was to guard the truth (1 Tim. 6:20; 2 Tim. 1:14) as well as proclaim it. That twofold responsibility is so basic, yet many preachers teach something other than God's Word. In Romans 10 Paul carefully explains the importance of emphasizing Scripture: "Whoever will call upon the name of the Lord will be saved. How then shall they call upon Him in whom they have not believed? And how shall they believe in Him whom they have not heard? And how shall they hear without a preacher? And how shall they preach unless they are sent? Just as it is written, 'How beautiful are the feet of those who bring glad tidings of good things!'. . . So faith comes from hearing, and hearing by the word of Christ" (vv. 13-15, 17).

Paul clearly was committed to proclaiming the Scriptures:

1. Colossians 1:25-27—"Of this church I was made a minister according to the stewardship from God bestowed on me for your benefit, that I might fully carry out the preaching of the word of God, that is, the mystery which has been hidden from the past ages and generations; but has now been manifested to His saints, to whom God willed to make known what is the riches of the glory of this mystery among the Gentiles, which is Christ in you, the hope of glory." The "mystery" Paul preached was the New Testament revelation.

2. 1 Corinthians 2:1-5—"When I came to you, brethren, I did not come with superiority of speech or of wisdom, proclaiming to you the testimony of God. For I determined to know nothing among you except Jesus Christ, and Him crucified. And I was with you in weakness and in fear and in much trembling. And my message and my preaching were not in persuasive words of wisdom, but in demonstration of the Spirit and of power, that your faith should not rest on the wisdom of men, but on the power of God."

3. 2 Corinthians 4:5—"We do not preach ourselves but Christ Jesus as Lord, and ourselves as your bond-servants for Jesus' sake."

By applying human reason, logic, and wisdom, gifted orators can move audiences by the power of their persuasive speech. But no man can be a faithful preacher without preaching the Word.

## The Only Way to Preach

Let me tell you why preaching the Word is the only way to preach.

1. It allows God to speak rather than man

When we preach the Word of *God*, we aren't preaching the word of man. Men can say things that are entertaining, interesting, informative, or even helpful. But it's imperative that you and I allow God to speak through His Word. One way God gives voice to His Word is through the preacher.

2. It brings the preacher into direct contact with the mind of the Holy Spirit

Since the Holy Spirit is the divine author of Scripture, digging deeply into the Word is like delving into the Holy Spirit's mind. For that reason, studying Scripture is even more exhilarating to me than preaching. Interacting with the Holy Spirit's reasoning, logic, and truth provides a tremendous time of communion with God. Expository preaching—a verse-by-verse explanation of Scripture—allows both the preacher and the listener to interact with the Holy Spirit's thoughts.

3. It forces the preacher to proclaim all the revelation of God

Expository preaching allows the preacher to declare "all the counsel of God" (Acts 20:27, KJV*). He will preach passages that convict him as well as his hearers. That produces integrity in his ministry.

*King James Version

4. It promotes biblical literacy

If the preacher told only interesting stories, you would know the stories, but not God's Word. However, the most important thing for you to hear is God's Word! I want to study and proclaim God's Word so that others can know it better. That should be your desire too.

5. It carries ultimate authority

The preacher's wisdom, voice, or demeanor might carry a certain amount of human authority, but it's no match for the divine authority of Scripture. If you want the Spirit to use you to compel people toward obedience, proclaim God's Word because it's the ultimate authority.

6. It transforms the preacher

The power of the Word is what the Holy Spirit uses to transform lives. If I only preached sermonettes, book reviews, entertaining stories, or simply the same message rehashed, God's Word wouldn't have an opportunity to interact with my life and transform me. And transformed preachers lead to transformed congregations.

Preaching the Word is what accomplishes God's work. In the 1800s William Taylor, pastor of the Broadway Tabernacle in New York City, wrote, "Let it never be forgotten, then, that he who would rise to eminence and usefulness in the pulpit, and become 'wise in winning souls,' must say of the work of the ministry, 'This one thing I do.' He must focus his whole heart and life upon the pulpit. He must give his days and his nights to the production of those addresses by which he seeks to convince the judgments, and move the hearts, and elevate the lives of his hearers" (*The Ministry of the Word* [N.Y.: Anson D. F. Randolph, 1876], p. 7). That convicts me because life offers so many distractions. And I believe those distractions are the main reason there aren't many powerful preachers today. The contemporary English preacher John Stott was right in saying we have many popular preachers but not many powerful ones.

## III. THE SCOPE OF THE PREACHER'S COMMISSION (v. 2b-f)

"Be ready in season and out of season; reprove, rebuke, exhort, with great patience and instruction."

### A. He Is Always Ready to Minister (v. 2b)

"Be ready in season and out of season."

Some translate the command "be urgent" or "be watchful." It pictures a military guard who is always at his post. It speaks of eagerness and describes someone who goes beyond his expected duty. The preacher has no set office hours but is always at his post ready to seize opportunities to preach the Word. That kind of compulsion to preach is evident throughout Scripture:

1. Jeremiah 20:8-9—The prophet said, "For me the word of the Lord has resulted in reproach and derision all day long. But if I say, 'I will not remember Him or speak anymore in His name,' then in my heart it becomes like a burning fire shut up in my bones; and I am weary of holding it in, and I cannot endure it." Jeremiah's reluctance to proclaim God's Word was overruled by a stronger inner compulsion to preach.

2. Romans 1:15—Paul said, "I am eager to preach the gospel to you also who are in Rome." He wanted Timothy to have that same eagerness.

3. Acts 21:11-13—The prophet Agabus "took Paul's belt and bound his own feet and hands, and said, 'This is what the Holy Spirit says: "In this way the Jews at Jerusalem will bind the man who owns this belt and deliver him into the hands of the Gentiles." ' " When the church heard this, they begged Paul not to go up to Jerusalem. But Paul replied, "What are you doing, weeping and breaking my heart? For I am ready not only to be bound, but even to die at Jerusalem for the name of the Lord Jesus." Not even the threat of death prevented Paul from preaching the Scriptures.

4. 1 Peter 3:15—Peter said, "Sanctify Christ as Lord in your hearts, always being ready to make a defense to everyone who asks you to give an account for the hope that is in you, yet with gentleness and reverence." We should always be ready to tell others about Christ.

Since there is no closed season on proclaiming Christ, we must make the most of every opportunity to tell others about Christ (cf. Eph. 5:16). Charles Spurgeon, a great preacher in London in the 1800s, said, "If I were asked— What in a Christian minister is the most essential quality for securing success in winning souls for Christ? I should reply, 'earnestness': and if I were asked a second or a third time, I should not vary the answer. . . . Success is proportionate to the preacher's earnestness" (*Lectures to My Students*, rev. ed. [Grand Rapids: Zondervan, 1978], p. 305). To preach you must have an earnestness and zeal that never dies.

But earnestness isn't a quality that comes naturally for the preacher or his listeners. After years of being exposed to sound preaching, the novelty of hearing God's Word can wear off, and the fire in the believer's heart can die out. It's exhilarating when both the teacher and the listener keep discovering what God's Word says. But we must not take preaching for granted and allow our hearts to become hard or apathetic.

Likewise the godly preacher must rely on the Holy Spirit's enabling when he preaches. In his *Journals and Letters* preacher John Wesley wrote, "I know that, were I *myself* to preach one whole year in one place, I should preach both myself and most of my congregation asleep" (cited in Spurgeon's *Lectures to My Students*, p. 309, emphasis added). Spurgeon himself said, "He, who at the end of twenty years' ministry among the same people is more alive than ever, is a great debtor to the quickening Spirit" (*Lectures to My Students*, p. 309). The believer's boldness and zeal will come through prayer and a diligent study of Scripture. As one Bible teacher said, "Study yourself to death and then pray yourself alive again." If you're communing with the Holy Spirit through prayer and the study of Scripture, you'll be zealous for God.

The pastor is to be ready to preach "in season and out of season" (2 Tim. 4:2). He is to preach when it's convenient and when it's not. His eagerness to preach must not depend on the receptivity of the audience to his message. Nothing is to constrain or silence his preaching of the Word.

## Standing for the Lord—Even at a Funeral

I heard of a funeral where Christians were instructed not to preach about Christ because many unbelievers would be present. Unfortunately, those Christians heeded that wrong advice out of fear. We, however, are to be faithful to God and tell others of His Word, not altering our message for the sake of social acceptance or the esteem of one's community. We aren't to be abusive or abrasive in what we say, but we are to be zealous in speaking the truth.

### B. He Exposes Sin (v. 2c)

"Reprove, rebuke."

The preacher is not only to be ready to preach, but also to reprove and rebuke sin. As 2 Timothy 3:16 says, "All Scripture is inspired by God and profitable . . . for reproof, for correction." In 2 Timothy 4:2 "reprove" speaks of being made aware of sin, while "rebuke" refers to the guilt that results from that awareness. Reproof uses God's Word to unveil sin. Rebuke is the Holy Spirit's convicting work through His Word.

Christ forcefully preached against sin (e.g., Matt. 15:1-9). John the Baptist was thrown in prison for doing so (Luke 3:19-20). We are to follow in their steps by exposing sin through the proclamation of God's Word. Ephesians 5:11 says not to "participate in the unfruitful deeds of darkness, but instead even expose them." Titus 1:13 says to "reprove [rebels] severely that they may be sound in the faith."

### C. He Encourages Right Behavior (v. 2d)

"Exhort."

The Greek term translated "exhort" (*parakaleō*) means "to encourage" and speaks of restoration. After confronting someone you know about sin, come alongside that individual and encourage positive steps toward change. That is what Paul did: "We were exhorting and encouraging and imploring each one of you as a father would his own children, so that you may walk in a manner worthy of the God who calls you into His own kingdom and glory" (1 Thess. 2:11-12). And that's what we're to do.

## D. He Is Patient (v. 2e)

"With great patience."

Patience is our guide as we reprove, rebuke, and exhort "Patience" (Gk., *makrothumia*) is used in connection with people, not events or circumstances. It's necessary to be patient with people because spiritual change usually takes time. If the recovery process takes longer than we like, it's tempting to be hard on the person, give up on him or her entirely, or pray that God might speedily send an unpleasant circumstance for chastisement. But the believer characterized by *makrothumia* isn't easily annoyed or irritated. He or she won't give way to bitterness or despair.

Patience is a spiritual grace—a gift from God that reflects His very nature. Paul asked, "Do you think lightly of the riches of [God's] kindness and forbearance and patience, not knowing that the kindness of God leads you to repentance?" (Rom. 2:4). Since God is patient with us, we must learn to be patient with each other (cf. Eph. 4:32).

## E. He Teaches Sound Doctrine (v. 2f)

"Instruction."

Paul said to expose sin and encourage others "with great patience and instruction" (Gk., *didachē*). We will help the unbeliever not only by pointing out his sin, but also by pointing him toward faith in God's Word. We will help another Christian not only by reproving his sin, but also by instructing him in righteousness (2 Tim. 3:16). Rebuke without instruction leaves people in the dark about what spiritual direction to take. Rebuke tells people where they shouldn't be, while instruction in doctrinal truth tells them where they should be.

## Conclusion

Not all believers are called to preach vocationally, but we all are called to give out the gospel (Matt. 28:18-20). Therefore we too are responsible to preach the Word eagerly whether in season or out. We also are to reprove and rebuke sin and then patiently instruct people toward righteousness. The preacher serves as a model of what you are to be. What he does in his unique way you are to do in your unique way. Since we all are responsible to the Judge, who will evaluate our faithfulness, together let's fulfill our glorious privilege of preaching the Word!

## Focusing on the Facts

1. In writing 2 Timothy 4:1-5 what does Paul want us to manifest before God and others (see p. 19-20)?
2. Explain the secular and biblical usage of the word translated "preach" in 2 Timothy 4:2 (see p. 21).
3. Explain why proclaiming God's Word might not have been an easy task for Timothy (see p. 21).
4. What specific error does Romans 10 refute (vv. 13-15, 17; see p. 22)?
5. No man can be a _____ preacher without preaching the Word (see p. 23).
6. What kind of interaction does expository preaching promote (see p. 23)?
7. What will mark the preacher's ministry with integrity (see pp. 23-24)?
8. What is the preacher's ultimate authority (see p. 24)?
9. What is one reason for the lack of power in the pulpit today (see p. 24)?
10. What picture does "be ready" portray in 2 Timothy 4:2? How does that apply to the preacher (see p. 25)?
11. What overruled the prophet Jeremiah's reluctance to preach (Jer. 20:8-9; see p. 25)?
12. What specific lesson does 1 Peter 3:15 teach (see pp. 25-26)?
13. How does "in season and out of season" apply to proclaiming God's Word (2 Tim. 4:2; see p. 26)?
14. What do "reprove," "rebuke," and "exhort" mean in 2 Timothy 4:2 (see pp. 27-28)?
15. Why is it necessary to exercise patience when reproving and exhorting someone (see p. 28)?
16. How do "rebuke" and "instruction" relate to each other (2 Tim. 4:2; see p. 28)?

## Pondering the Principles

1. God's Word is the only message you are to proclaim. Look up the following verses to see what they say about God's Word. Meditate on the truths they teach and ask the Lord to give you a deeper appreciation for His Word.

- Jeremiah 15:16; 1 Peter 2:2

- Isaiah 40:8; 1 Peter 1:23-25

- Psalm 12:6; 19:8

- Jeremiah 23:29; Hebrews 4:12

- Psalm 119:9; John 15:3

- Proverbs 6:23; 2 Peter 1:19

2. The commands to reprove, rebuke, and exhort are a call for you to be involved in other people's lives. Accept your responsibility to confront sin and teach sound doctrine in love. Doing so will help others stand strong in the Lord. Conversely, be open to reproof and instruction from other believers. If what they say agrees with Scripture, gratefully accept their counsel. Proverbs 25:12 says, "Like an earring of gold and an ornament of fine gold is a wise reprover to a listening ear." Proverbs 9:8-9 says, "Reprove a wise man, and he will love you. Give instruction to a wise man, and he will be still wiser, teach a righteous man, and he will increase his learning." Let the truth of those verses be reflected in your life.

# 3

# Marks of the Faithful Preacher—Part 3

## Outline

Introduction
A. A Call to Spiritual Commitment
B. A Call to Spiritual Excellence

Review
I.   The Seriousness of the Preacher's Commission (v. 1)
II.  The Essence of the Preacher's Commission (v. 2a)
III. The Scope of the Preacher's Commission (v. 2b-f)

Lesson
IV. The Urgency of the Preacher's Commission (vv. 3-4)
    A. The Unbeliever's Intolerance of Truth (v. 3)
       1. What he doesn't want to hear
       2. What he does want to hear
    B. The Unbeliever's Appetite for False Teaching (v. 4)
V.  The Attitude Undergirding the Preacher's Commission (v. 5a)

Conclusion

## Introduction

### A. A Call to Spiritual Commitment

In 1 and 2 Timothy Paul gave a breadth of responsibility to Timothy. Timothy was to correct those who taught false doctrine. He was to call people to a pure heart, a good conscience, and a sincere faith. He was to fight for divine truth and God's purposes. He was to pray for the lost and lead those in the church to do the same. He was to call women to fulfill their God-given roles of submission and rearing godly children through faith, love, holiness.

Timothy was to exercise care in selecting godly men for church leadership. He was to nourish believers continually through preaching God's Word. He was to discipline himself in godliness so that others could follow his example. He was to read, explain, and apply the Scriptures publicly. He was to progress toward Christlikeness. He was to be gracious and gentle in confronting sin. He was to give special consideration and care to widows. He was to honor faithful pastors who work hard and not receive an accusation against any of them unless it was substantiated by two or three witnesses.

Timothy was to care for his health that he might have strength to minister. He was to flee the love of money, but pursue righteousness, godliness, faith, love, perseverance, and gentleness. He was to fight for the faith in the midst of hostile opposition. He was to obey the Lord's commandments and guard His Word as a sacred trust. He was to keep his spiritual gift fresh and useful and not be timid. He was not to be ashamed of Christ or those who serve Him. He was to reproduce himself in faithful men.

Timothy also was to expect and willingly accept suffering and persecution for the sake of Christ. He was to keep his eyes on Christ at all times. He was to exercise leadership with authority. He was to interpret and apply Scripture accurately. He was to avoid useless conversations. He was to be an instrument of honor by setting himself apart from sin. He was to flee sinful desires. And he wasn't to be contentious but teachable, gentle, and patient—even when wronged.

Paul's charge was not only to Timothy but to anyone who ministers. Fulfilling that charge requires commitment, but it's been well said that "the only true happiness comes from squandering ourselves for a great purpose" (John Mason Brown, cited in John W. Gardner's *Excellence* [N.Y.: Harper & Row, 1961], p. 149). The supreme purpose in life is to glorify God. Those who give of themselves for that great cause receive back the highest sense of fulfillment.

## B. A Call to Spiritual Excellence

Giving Timothy such a breadth of responsibility was a call to spiritual excellence. Paul never measured Timothy's spiritual excellence by the size of a church or the amount of money it took in. Neither did he consider the world's acceptance of Timothy. That's because Paul made a distinction between spiritual excellence and worldly success.

Jon Johnston explored the differences between excellence and success in his book *Christian Excellence: Alternative to Success* (Grand Rapids: Baker, 1985). He suggested that success and excellence are competing ideals, defining success as attaining cultural goals that elevate one's importance in society. Status in one's culture usually brings four things: power, prestige, wealth, and privilege. Power refers to one's sphere of influence or domination, prestige speaks of being esteemed or honored, wealth refers to an abundance of money, and privilege refers to being able to do what most can't.

In contrast, Johnston described excellence as the pursuit of quality in one's work and effort. And that pursuit doesn't depend on having one's effort recognized by others. Success seeks status, but excellence seeks satisfaction. Success is in relation to others, but excellence is in relation to one's potential. Success is being esteemed by people, excellence is being the best you can be. Worldly success seeks to please men, but spiritual excellence seeks to please God.

Johnston then offered this comparison: "Success offers a hoped-for future goal. Excellence provides a striven-for present standard. Success bases our worth on a comparison with others. Excellence gauges our value by measuring us against our own potential. Success grants its rewards to the few but is the dream of the multitudes. Excellence is available to all living beings but is accepted by the special few. Success focuses its attention on the external—becoming the tastemaker for the insatiable appetites of the conspicuous consumer.

"Excellence beams its spotlight on the internal spirit—becoming the quiet but pervasive conscience of the conscientious who yearn for integrity. Success engenders fantasy and a compulsive groping for the pot of gold at the end of the rainbow. Excellence brings us to reality and a deep gratitude for [the promise of joy when we do our best]. Success encourages expedience and compromise, which prompts us to treat people as means to our end. Excellence cultivates principles and consistency, which ensure that we will treat all persons as intrinsically valuable ends—the apex of our heavenly Father's creation" (p. 33).

Excellence deals with your character and integrity. Success often involves lying, cheating, or stealing. You can obtain success by cheap discounts, but you must pay the full price for excellence. Johnston quoted David Neff as saying, "Success is the key they hand you when they like you. It doesn't matter why. They just give you the key that unlocks an upscale condo, triggers the powerful purr of your new Mercedes, and accesses the executive washroom. It's what they give you.

"Excellence is [different]. It's what's within you. It's what you do that stretches mind and muscle. They'll hand you success when your ratings are up, your sales soar, or when the eager masses plunk down their grubby bucks to buy your stuff. And they'll snatch success away at daybreak. Success loves its one-night stands at the Ritz. But never expect it to say, I do. Success is a day-tripper and a tease. [Success will] forget you. Excellence endures when the crowd moves on" (p. 8).

What honestly motivates you: worldly success or spiritual excellence? Pride is the source of success, but humility is the source of excellence. Excellence says, "I'm content to be the best I can be." Success says, "I'm not content until I'm better than you."

## Annihilation by Exaltation

We must learn to be content in God's will. That is well illustrated in a story I read about a delicate little watch that was dissatisfied with being in a lady's pocket. It envied Big Ben, the great tower clock in London. As the little watch accompanied the lady aboard a ship crossing under the Westminster Bridge—in full view of Big Ben—this exchange took place:

"I wish I could be up there," said the little delicate watch. "Then I could serve a multitude of people."

"You shall have your opportunity, little watch," responded the ship's tour guide.

The little watch was then drawn up to the tower by a slender thread. When it reached the top, the guide said, "Where are you, little watch? I cannot see you." After a dramatic pause, the guide then said, "Its elevation has become its annihilation." We most effectively serve the Lord when we accept His design for our lives.

In 2 Timothy 4:1-5 Paul gives several requirements to help us live up to our God-given potential and achieve spiritual excellence.

## Review

I. THE SERIOUSNESS OF THE PREACHER'S COMMISSION (v. 1; see pp. 10-15)

A. His Compelling Responsibility (v. 1a; see pp. 10-11)

B. His Coming Evaluation (v. 1b; see pp. 12-15)

II. THE ESSENCE OF THE PREACHER'S COMMISSION (v. 2a; see pp. 20-24)

A. Timothy's Character (see p. 21)

B. Timothy's Message (see pp. 22-23)

III. THE SCOPE OF THE PREACHER'S COMMISSION (v. 2b-f; see pp. 25-28)

A. He Is Always Ready to Minister (v. 2b; see pp. 25-26)

B. He Exposes Sin (v. 2c; see p. 27)

C. He Encourages Right Behavior (v. 2d; see pp. 27-28)

D. He Is Patient (v. 2e; see p. 28)

E. He Teaches Sound Doctrine (v. 2f; see p. 28)

One old creed well stated that the minister is to preach no sacrifice but Calvary, no priest but Christ, no confessional but the throne of grace, and no authority but the Word of God. His preaching ought to be interesting to listen to, clear to understand, and practical to make biblical application for obedience.

## Lesson

IV. THE URGENCY OF THE PREACHER'S COMMISSION
(vv. 3-4)

"The time will come when they will not endure sound doctrine; but wanting to have their ears tickled, they will accumulate for themselves teachers in accordance to their own desires; and will turn away their ears from the truth, and will turn aside to myths."

A. The Unbeliever's Intolerance of Truth (v. 3)

"The time will come when they will not endure sound doctrine; but wanting to have their ears tickled, they will accumulate for themselves teachers in accordance to their own desires."

1. What he doesn't want to hear

"The time will come" introduces a prediction similar to 1 Timothy 4:1: "The Spirit explicitly says that in later times some will fall away from the faith, paying attention to deceitful spirits and doctrines of demons." Second Timothy 3:1 says, "In the last days difficult times will come." The Greek word used in all three incidents (*kairos*) refers to an epoch or season. Throughout church history there have been times when people didn't want to hear God's Word.

Christ spoke to His disciples about those who would reject the truth: "I send you out as sheep in the midst of wolves; therefore be shrewd as serpents, and innocent as doves. But beware of men; for they will deliver you up to the courts, and scourge you in their synagogues; and you shall even be brought before governors and kings for My sake, as a testimony to them and to the Gentiles. But when they deliver you up, do not become anxious about how or what you will speak; for it shall be given you in that hour what you are to speak. For it is not you who speak, but it is the Spirit of your Father who speaks in you.

36

"And brother will deliver up brother to death, and a father his child; and children will rise up against parents, and cause them to be put to death. And you will be hated by all on account of My name, but it is the one who has endured to the end who will be saved. But whenever they persecute you in this city, flee to the next; for truly I say to you, you shall not finish going through the cities of Israel, until the Son of Man comes" (Matt. 10:16-23). The world not only rejects God's Word, but also persecutes those who proclaim it. Christ also told His disciples: "They will make you outcasts from the synagogue, but an hour is coming for everyone who kills you to think that he is offering service to God" (John 16:2).

The lost react that way because they can't "endure sound doctrine" (2 Tim. 4:3). The Greek word *anechō* means "to hold up" or "bear with" and can be translated "to tolerate." First Timothy 1:10 describes those who turn a deaf ear to avoid biblical teaching as "immoral men and homosexuals and kidnappers and liars and perjurers." However, 2 Timothy 4:3 refers not only to those outside the professing church but also to those inside it. Timothy preached to both groups.

In the Ephesian church where Timothy was ministering, some had no interest in God's Word. In the days of the prophet Isaiah only one-tenth of the people wanted to hear his message (Isa. 6:13). It's no different in today's professing church. That's because the lost have ears that are dull, eyes that are dim, and hearts that are insensitive (6:10).

## Ravenous Wolves in Sheep's Clothing

There was a time when our country honored God's Word and respected the minister. But that's not true anymore. In fact, it's not only the world that's despising the truth, but also the professing church. Within the large framework of professing Christendom a small remnant of true believers eagerly hear sound teaching. But some of the lost in the professing church support such things as homosexual and feminist causes. There is even a so-called Bible that has removed masculine references to God to avoid offending feminist beliefs.

The lost, whether outside or inside the professing church, refuse to hear God's teaching about controversial issues such as the woman's role, homosexuality, or abortion. They won't tolerate strong biblical teaching because it confronts and refutes their errors and calls for their obedience. By adopting the ways of the world, much of the professing church has become corrupt and perverse. Apart from a dramatic change, the pressure will continue to intensify against those who speak the truth.

### 2. What he does want to hear

The lost, "wanting to have their ears tickled . . . will accumulate for themselves teachers in accordance to their own desires" (2 Tim. 4:3). Unbelievers want a teacher to say only what they want to hear. In the days of the prophet Jeremiah the people were the same way: "An appalling and horrible thing has happened in the land: The prophets prophesy falsely, and the priests rule on their own authority; and My people love it so!" (Jer. 5:30-31). The people wanted the prophets to lie and the priests to forsake divine authority.

The prophet Ezekiel received similar opposition: "As for you, [Ezekiel], your fellow citizens who talk about you by the walls and in the doorways of the houses, speak to one another, each to his brother, saying, 'Come now, and hear what the message is which comes forth from the Lord.' And they come to you as people come, and sit before you as My people, and hear your words, but they do not do them, for they do the lustful desires expressed by their mouth, and their heart goes after their gain.

"And behold, you are to them like a sensual song by one who has a beautiful voice and plays well on an instrument; for they hear your words, but they do not practice them. So when it comes to pass—as surely it will—then they will know that a prophet has been in their midst" (Ezek. 33:30-33). The people received Ezekiel's message as mere oratorical entertainment.

Second Timothy 4:3 tells us the ungodly amass teachers according to their own "desires" (Gk., *epithumia*). Here the word refers to sinful lusts. Churches today are filled with so-called preachers who say only what the congregation wants to hear. Such congregations are like the philosophers in ancient Athens who spent their time "in nothing other than telling or hearing something new" (Acts 17:21). The attitude of the lost is,

"Make me feel good about myself. Tell me something sensational, entertaining, or that builds up my ego."

Not surprisingly, those same people will reject biblical messages that expose their sins. But the preacher they least like to hear brings the message they most need to hear. As Bible scholar Marvin Vincent pointed out, "If the people desire a calf to worship, a ministerial calf-maker is readily found" (*Word Studies in the New Testament*, vol. 4 [New York: Charles Scribner's Sons, 1903], p. 321). How sad that is!

B. The Unbeliever's Appetite for False Teaching (v. 4)

"[They] will turn away their ears from the truth, and will turn aside to myths."

Verse 3 shows that many unbelievers will deliberately refuse the truth, while verse 4 reveals them to be victims of their wrong choice. Instead of wanting to hear God's Word, they'd rather hear hypocritical liars who function as agents of Satan. Their turning away from Scripture lays them open to Satan's influence so that they are easily turned to error. The Greek verb translated "will turn aside" (*ektrepō*) speaks of twisting or dislocating. Their minds become dislocated, out of joint, or non-functioning because they believe myths.

The Greek term translated "myths" (*muthos*) literally means "fables" and speaks of false teaching. The lost amass or heap up for themselves false teachers to "have their ears tickled" (v. 3). They prefer to be entertained by teachings that produce pleasant sensations and leave them with a good feeling. They have an itch to get their ears tickled by nice stories, positive thinking, and a little psychology. However, the gospel doesn't tickle the ears—it boxes them! Only then will salvation follow. God's Word brings reproof, rebuke, and conviction of sin. Therefore, it's imperative that we continue to proclaim God's Word to the lost.

## Vetoing the Valedictorian

I read about a young girl in high school who was the valedictorian of her school's senior class. As a Christian she wanted to honor the Lord in her commencement address by saying, "The most important Person in my life is the Lord." But school officials demanded that she remove the word *Lord* from her speech. She refused and therefore the school would not allow her to speak. That happened in the United States of America! Our coins are printed with "In God we trust," yet a young person was forbidden to say "Lord" in a public address. In some ways our country has an intolerance for biblical truth. So it's important that we make the most of our opportunities to give out the Word while we can.

## V. THE ATTITUDE UNDERGIRDING THE PREACHER'S COMMISSION (v. 5a)

"But you, be sober in all things."

"But you" introduces a contrast to the ungodly who reject God's Word. "Sober" means "self-contained" or "steady" and speaks of someone who is stable, unwavering, and steadfast. Bible scholar Fenton Hort described it as a mental state where "every faculty [is] at full command, to look all facts and all considerations deliberately in the face" (cited by William Barclay in *The Letters to Timothy, Titus, and Philemon*, rev. ed. [Philadelphia: Westminster, 1975], p. 207). The sober person is like an athlete who brings all his passions, appetites, and nerves under complete control for maximum performance. The opposite is someone who is flaky, trendy, whimsical, or inconsistent.

We don't need flaky, trendy, or whimsical preachers whose messages coincide with the latest fancies of the lost. In the midst of our chaotic and changing world we need preachers whose heads are clear of such things and unaffected by people's desire to have their ears tickled. I believe "sober" also implies an unruffled alertness or watchfulness. The mind of the sober believer is balanced with biblical truth and unswayed by the sinful desires of the lost.

### Conclusion

Paul's call to spiritual excellence was not only for Timothy, but also for all believers. If you strive for worldly success, you'll be like that little pocket watch—useless to God and others. Pursuing worldly success will lead you to compromise the truth, but pursuing spiritual excellence will keep you strong. You can travel the cheap route of worldly success or travel the costly route of spiritual excellence. The reward for worldly success is earthly and temporal, but the reward for spiritual excellence is heavenly and eternal.

## Focusing on the Facts

1. What did fulfilling Paul's charge require of Timothy (see pp. 32-33)?
2. Summarize the differences between success and excellence (see pp. 33-34).
3. What was Christ teaching His disciples in Matthew 10:16-23 (see p. 37)?
4. Whom does 2 Timothy 4:3 refer to (see p. 37)?
5. What was Isaiah's description of the lost (Isa. 6:10; see pp. 37-38)?
6. Why has much of the professing church become corrupt and perverse (see p. 38)?
7. What was the reaction of the people to God's Word in the days of Jeremiah and Ezekiel (Jer. 5:30-31; Ezek. 33:30-33; see pp. 38-39)?
8. What does "desires" refer to in 2 Timothy 4:3? How does that apply to today's church (see p. 39)?
9. The preacher unbelievers _____ like to hear brings the message they _____ need to hear (see p. 39).
10. What is the distinction between 2 Timothy 4:3 and 4:4 (see p. 39)?
11. In rejecting God's Word, whose influence will the lost be under? What will that turn them to (see p. 39)?
12. What happens to the mind of the unbelieving when they "turn aside" from the truth (2 Tim. 4:4; see p. 39)?
13. What do "myths" refer to in 2 Timothy 4:4 (see p. 40)?
14. How do the lost "have their ears tickled" (2 Tim. 4:3; see p. 40)?
15. What does "sober" mean in 2 Timothy 4:5? Who is the sober person like (see p. 40)?
16. The call to spiritual excellence is for _____ (see p. 41).

## Pondering the Principles

1. The lost have an intolerance of truth and an appetite for false teaching. But as a Christian you should have an insatiable appetite for truth and an abhorrence for false teaching. Look up the following verses and then write out the principles they teach about truth and falsehood:

- Psalm 101:7

- Proverbs 12:22

- Zechariah 8:16

- Malachi 2:6

- John 18:37

- Ephesians 4:25

- Revelation 21:8

2.  In spite of increasing opposition to God and His Word, be spiritually steadfast. Moses exemplified such an attitude. Hebrews 11:24-27 tells us he "refused to be called the son of Pharaoh's daughter; choosing rather to endure ill-treatment with the people of God, than to enjoy the passing pleasures of sin; considering the reproach of Christ greater riches than the treasures of Egypt; for he was looking to the reward. By faith he left Egypt, not fearing the wrath of the king; for he endured, as seeing Him who is unseen." Moses could have chosen honor, riches, and pleasure in the court of Egypt, but he refused to do so. Instead he chose scorn, suffering, and affliction for the sake of God and His people. In the face of Pharaoh's wrath Moses's heart was steadfast in faith and firmly fixed on the unseen One. Ask the Lord to help you be steadfast like Moses.

# 4

# Marks of the Faithful Preacher—Part 4

## Outline

Introduction
A. Whom the Lord Calls into Ministry
  1. His general call to all believers
  2. His specific call to some believers
B. How the Lord Calls Particular Ministers
  1. He calls subjectively
  2. He calls objectively
  3. He calls collectively
  4. He calls effectively

Review
  I.   The Seriousness of the Preacher's Commission (v. 1)
  II.  The Essence of the Preacher's Commission (v. 2a)
  III. The Scope of the Preacher's Commission (v. 2b-f)
  IV.  The Urgency of the Preacher's Commission (vv. 3-4)
  V.   The Attitude Undergirding the Preacher's Commission (v. 5a)

Lesson
  VI.   The Cost of the Preacher's Commission (v. 5b)
        A. Expect Suffering
        B. Accept Suffering
  VII.  The Extent of the Preacher's Commission (v. 5c)
  VIII. The Goal of the Preacher's Commission (v. 5d)

## Introduction

The dominant element of 1 and 2 Timothy is a series of commands that Paul gave to Timothy. What makes those commands binding not only on Timothy but also on all preachers and teachers is the call of God. What is the call of God? To find out let's look more closely at that subject.

A. Whom the Lord Calls into Ministry

   1. His general call to all believers

   Scripture affirms that all believers are to proclaim Christ.

   a) Ephesians 2:10—"We are His workmanship, created in Christ Jesus for good works, which God prepared beforehand, that we should walk in them." We are saved for the purpose of doing good works, which include evangelizing the lost.

   b) Revelation 22:17—"The Spirit and the bride say, 'Come.' And let the one who hears say, 'Come.' And let the one who is thirsty come; let the one who wishes take the water of life without cost." All who hear and accept God's invitation for salvation are responsible to proclaim the gospel to others.

   c) 1 Peter 2:9—"You are a chosen race, a royal priesthood, a holy nation, a people for God's own possession, that you may proclaim the excellencies of Him who has called you out of darkness into His marvelous light." God's people are to proclaim Christ to others.

   d) Deuteronomy 11:13—"Love the Lord your God and . . . serve Him with all your heart and all your soul." Our love and service to the Lord includes evangelizing the lost.

   e) 2 Corinthians 5:20—"We are ambassadors for Christ, as though God were entreating through us; we beg you on behalf of Christ, be reconciled to God." All believers are responsible to urge the lost to come to Christ.

   Charles Spurgeon wrote, "The propagation of the gospel is left, not to a few, but to all the disciples of the Lord Jesus Christ: according to the measure of grace entrusted to him by the Holy Spirit, each man is bound to minister in his day and generation, both to the church and among unbelievers. . . . [All Christians are] to exert themselves to the utmost to extend the knowledge of the

Lord Jesus Christ" (*Lectures to My Students* [Grand Rapids: Zondervan, 1978], p. 22).

All believers have the worthy call of exalting Christ and extending His kingdom (Eph. 4:1). By exercising our spiritual gifts each of us can serve Christ and His people.

2. His specific call to some believers

God also calls some men to minister vocationally. Throughout Scripture that has always been God's way.

a) Exodus 28:3—The Lord said to Moses, "You shall speak to all the skillful persons whom I have endowed with the spirit of wisdom, that they make Aaron's garments to consecrate him, that he may minister as priest to Me." Aaron, the brother of Moses, was to be properly cared for because God had set him apart as the high priest of Israel.

b) Isaiah 6:8-9—Isaiah said, "I heard the voice of the Lord, saying, 'Whom shall I send, and who will go for Us?' Then I said, 'Here am I. Send me!' And [The Lord] said, 'Go, and tell this people.' " The Lord called Isaiah to proclaim His message to the nation Israel.

c) Jeremiah 1:5—The Lord said to Jeremiah, "Before I formed you in the womb I knew you, and before you were born I consecrated you; I have appointed you a prophet to the nations."

d) Jeremiah 3:15—The Lord said to the nation Israel, "I will give you shepherds after My own heart, who will feed you on knowledge and understanding."

e) Ezekiel 2:3-4, 7—The Lord said to Ezekiel, "Son of man, I am sending you to the sons of Israel, to a rebellious people who have rebelled against Me; they and their fathers have transgressed against Me to this very day. And I am sending you to them who are stubborn and obstinate children; and you shall say to them, 'Thus says the Lord God.'. . . You shall speak My words to them whether they listen or not, for they are rebellious."

*f)* Acts 9:15—The Lord said, "[Paul] is a chosen instrument of Mine, to bear My name before the Gentiles and kings and the sons of Israel."

*g)* Ephesians 4:11-12—The Lord "gave some as apostles, and some as prophets, and some as evangelists, and some as pastors and teachers, for the equipping of the saints for the work of service, to the building up of the body of Christ."

*h)* Colossians 1:23, 25—"Continue in the faith firmly established and steadfast, and not moved away from the hope of the gospel that you have heard, which was proclaimed in all creation under heaven, and of which I, Paul, was made a minister. . . . Of this church I was made a minister according to the stewardship from God bestowed on me for your benefit, that I might fully carry out the preaching of the word of God."

*i)* 1 Timothy 1:12; 2:7; 2 Timothy 1:11—Paul said, "I thank Christ Jesus our Lord, who has strengthened me, because He considered me faithful, putting me into service. . . . I was appointed a preacher and an apostle (I am telling the truth, I am not lying) as a teacher of the Gentiles in faith and truth. . . . I was appointed a preacher and an apostle and a teacher."

God also called Timothy to preach, and in Acts 16:1-4 we see him beginning to minister alongside Paul.

B. How the Lord Calls Particular Ministers

How can a man know if the Lord has called him to preach? I believe Scripture indicates four ways he can know.

1. He calls subjectively

I believe that men who are called to preach are internally compelled to do so by the Holy Spirit. Spurgeon described that compulsion as "an irresistible, overwhelming craving and raging thirst for telling to others what God has done to our own souls" (*Lectures to My Students*, p. 26). Paul said it this way: "If I preach the gospel, I have nothing to boast of, for I am under compulsion; for woe is me if I do not preach the gospel. For if I do this voluntarily, I have a reward; but if against my will, I have a stewardship entrusted to me" (1 Cor. 9:16-17).

Now compulsion isn't necessarily the same as ambition. Ambition usually stems from our own desires to fulfill certain established goals and dreams. But compulsion is generated by an external source—in this case the Holy Spirit. The Holy Spirit is the One who gives a man the compulsion to preach "for the sake of the Name" (3 John 7) and aspire to the office of an elder (1 Tim. 3:1).

Certainly Joseph Alleine, a Puritan pastor and author of *An Alarm to the Unconverted,* had an inner compulsion from God to preach. It was said that "he was infinitely and insatiably greedy [for] the conversion of souls" (cited by Spurgeon in *Lectures to My Students,* p. 26). His spiritual passion for reaching the lost resulted in his being imprisoned on numerous occasions. In poor health, he died at the age of thirty-four.

I believe Scripture indicates that Timothy also had a spiritual compulsion to preach. Otherwise Paul wouldn't have mentioned him as his partner in ministry: "Paul, an apostle of Christ Jesus by the will of God, and Timothy our brother, to the church of God which is at Corinth with all the saints who are throughout Achaia" (2 Cor. 1:1). Throughout the rest of that chapter, Paul used the pronoun "we" because Timothy was his colaborer in ministry. In verse 19 he directly refers to Timothy's preaching Christ.

I believe Philippians 2:19-22 also indicates Timothy's spiritual compulsion to minister, for Paul said, "I hope in the Lord Jesus to send Timothy to you shortly, so that I also may be encouraged when I learn of your condition. For I have no one else of kindred spirit who will genuinely be concerned for your welfare. For they all seek after their own interests, not those of Christ Jesus. But you know of his proven worth that he served with me in the furtherance of the gospel like a child serving his father." Both Paul and the Philippian church knew of Timothy's faithfulness in proclaiming the gospel.

## Entering the Ministry for the Right Reason

In lecturing to his students at the Pastor's College, Spurgeon said, "If any student in this room could be content to be a newspaper editor, or a grocer, or a farmer, or a doctor, or a lawyer, or a senator, or a king, in the name of heaven and earth let him go his way; he is not the man in whom dwells the Spirit of God in its fulness, for a man so filled with God would utterly weary of any pursuit but that for which his inmost soul pants.

"If on the other hand, you can say that for all the wealth of both the Indies you could not and dare not espouse any other calling so as to be put aside from preaching the gospel of Jesus Christ, then, depend upon it, if other things be equally satisfactory, you have the signs of this apostleship. We must feel that woe is unto us if we preach not the gospel; the Word of God must be unto us as fire in our bones, otherwise, if we undertake the ministry, we shall be unhappy in it, shall be unable to bear the self-denials incident to it, and shall be of little service to those among whom we minister.

"I speak of self-denials, and well I may; for the true pastor's work is full of them, and without a love to his calling he will soon succumb, and either leave the drudgery, or move on in discontent, burdened with a monotony as tiresome as that of a blind horse in a mill" (*Lectures to My Students*, pp. 26-27). If you would enter the ministry, be certain you are called to do so.

2.  He calls objectively

    Today God doesn't call his messengers with a voice from heaven as He did with Paul or some of the Old Testament prophets. Instead He links His subjective call to objective factors such as a man's circumstances and spiritual giftedness. God will make His call evident by giving a man spiritual wisdom, courage, an affection for God's people, and an ability to lead. So God's call begins with a compulsion and then takes shape through His providential ordering of a man's experiences and abilities.

    John Newton wrote, "That which finally evidences a proper call, is a correspondent opening in providence, by a gradual train of circumstances pointing out the means, the time, the place, of actually entering upon the work" (cited by Spurgeon in *Lectures to My Students*, p. 34). That was Timothy's experience. In Acts

16 Paul identified Timothy as a young man he wanted to train for the ministry. Undoubtedly that happened as a result of God's providential ordering of circumstances.

Later Timothy was ordained for the ministry (1 Tim. 4:14). His circumstances, opportunities for ministry, and spiritual giftedness had been in place, by God's design, for some time. If God calls you to preach, He will do the same for you.

## 3. He calls collectively

Collectively the church must evaluate a man's character to see if he meets the qualifications of 1 Timothy 3:2-7: "above reproach, the husband of one wife, temperate, prudent, respectable, hospitable, able to teach, not addicted to wine or pugnacious, but gentle, uncontentious, free from the love of money.

"He must be one who manages his own household well, keeping his children under control with all dignity (but if a man does not know how to manage his own household, how will he take care of the church of God?); and not a new convert, lest he become conceited and fall into the condemnation incurred by the devil. And he must have a good reputation with those outside the church, so that he may not fall into reproach and the snare of the devil" (cf. Titus 1:6-9).

A man might believe he is motivated and gifted for the ministry, but he might not have a godly character. That's why it's necessary for the church to hold him accountable. In Acts 13:1-3 the church affirmed Paul and Barnabas for their missionary work. In 1 Timothy 4:14 the church elders laid hands on Timothy in recognition of his call to the ministry (cf. 2 Tim. 1:6). God follows that same pattern today. If He calls you to preach, your church will be able to affirm your spiritual gifts and character.

## 4. He calls effectively

The man whom God calls to preach will also have an effective ministry. First Thessalonians 2:1 reveals that Paul and Timothy's ministry in Thessalonica "was not in vain." Paul affirmed and complemented the effectiveness of Timothy's ministry by saying, "He is doing the Lord's work, as I also am" (1 Cor. 16:10). If you believe you have a spiritual compulsion and giftedness to minister, you still need to ask yourself, *Has my present ministry in the church been effective? Do sinners face conviction? Do saints grow?*

Since the Lord called Timothy to preach, Paul instructed him about being a faithful minister in 2 Timothy 4:1-5. In those verses we find the marks of a faithful preacher and teacher.

## Review

I. THE SERIOUSNESS OF THE PREACHER'S COMMISSION (v. 1; see pp. 10-15)

   A. His Compelling Responsibility (v. 1*a*; see pp. 10-11)

   B. His Coming Evaluation (v. 1*b*; see pp. 12-15)

II. THE ESSENCE OF THE PREACHER'S COMMISSION (v. 2*a*; see pp. 20-24)

III. THE SCOPE OF THE PREACHER'S COMMISSION (v. 2*b-d*; see pp. 25-28)

IV. THE URGENCY OF THE PREACHER'S COMMISSION (vv. 3-4; see pp. 36-40)

   A. The Unbeliever's Intolerance of Truth (v. 3; see pp. 36-39)

   B. The Unbeliever's Appetite for False Teaching (v. 4; see pp. 39-40)

V. THE ATTITUDE UNDERGIRDING THE PREACHER'S COMMISSION (v. 5*a*; see pp. 40-41)

## VI. THE COST OF THE PREACHER'S COMMISSION (v. 5*b*)

"Endure hardship."

### A. Expect Suffering

Many preachers want a ministry free of difficulties. However, I believe faithfulness to God's Word and the endurance of trials are the marks of an effective ministry. A preacher has the choice of either enduring or compromising a difficult situation. That's why Paul told Timothy, "You therefore, my son, be strong in the grace that is in Christ Jesus. . . . Suffer hardship with me, as a good soldier of Christ Jesus" (2 Tim. 2:1, 3). Timothy knew that "difficult times" would come (2 Tim. 3:1) and that some would "fall away from the faith" (1 Tim. 4:1). Nevertheless, he was to follow the steps of Paul and fight "the good fight" (2 Tim. 4:7).

### B. Accept Suffering

Timothy not only expected suffering, but also willingly accepted it. The writer of the book of Hebrews said, "Take notice that our brother Timothy has been released, with whom, if he comes soon, I shall see you" (13:23). Here the Greek verb translated "released" (*apoluō*) speaks of releasing someone from prison. Apparently Timothy was imprisoned for preaching Christ. Since it's likely Hebrews was written soon after 2 Timothy, Timothy may have been jailed while ministering in Ephesus, shortly after receiving 2 Timothy. Like Timothy, we also are to endure whatever rejection, hostility, and persecution that comes from following Christ.

## VII. THE EXTENT OF THE PREACHER'S COMMISSION (v. 5*c*)

"Do the work of an evangelist."

The Greek term translated "evangelist" (*euaggelistēs*) is mentioned only here and two other times in the New Testament (Acts 21:8; Eph. 4:11). However, the verb *euaggelizō*, which means "to proclaim good news," is mentioned over fifty times. And the noun *euaggelion*, which means "good news" or "gospel," is mentioned over seventy times. Preaching the gospel to the lost has a significant place in the New Testament.

Evangelists are proclaimers of the good news and often serve in places where Christ is not named. Here in 2 Timothy 4:5 "evangelist" occurs without the definite article and therefore is a general reference to an evangelist's work or function.

## Advice on How to Proclaim God's Word

In preaching I believe there are two important things to remember.

1. Make your message simple and clear

   Don't try to impress people with your erudition or extensive Bible knowledge. There's no virtue in making a message hard to understand. Notice the simplistic beauty of this familiar rhyme:

   > Twinkle, twinkle, little star,
   > How I wonder what you are,
   > Up above the world so high,
   > Like a diamond in the sky.

2. Rely on God, not on manipulative techniques

   Preaching calls for a response from those who hear God's Word, but don't try to manipulate that response. Unfortunately, some churches do just that by using lilting music and dim lights right after the message has been preached. They've been told that such techniques make it easier for people to believe God's Word. But Martyn Lloyd-Jones, the pastor of Westminster Chapel in London for many years, correctly labeled those manipulative tactics as "psychological conditioning" (*Preaching and Preachers* [Grand Rapids: Zondervan, 1971], p. 268). God alone, not lilting music and dim lights, causes one to believe in Scripture.

   Lloyd-Jones went on to say, "You should not put direct pressure on the will. The will should always be approached primarily through the mind, the intellect, and then through the affections. . . . As the mind grasps [God's Word and], understands it, the affections are kindled and moved, and so in turn the will is persuaded and obedience is the outcome. . . . Obedience is not the result of direct pressure on the will, it is the result of an enlightened mind and a softened heart" (p. 271).

The use of manipulative evangelistic techniques implies "sinners have an inherent power of decision and of self-conversion. But that cannot be reconciled with scriptural teaching such as . . . Ephesians 2:1, 'You hath He quickened, who were dead in trespasses and sins.' ". . . There is an implication here "that the evangelist somehow is in a position to manipulate the Holy Spirit and His work. The evangelist has but to appear and to make his appeal and the results follow inevitably. . . . [That] tends to produce a superficial conviction of sin. . . . A sinner does not 'decide' for Christ; the sinner 'flies' to Christ in utter helplessness and despair. . . . No man truly comes to Christ unless he flies to Him as his only refuge and hope" (pp. 279-80).

Timothy was to "do the work of an evangelist" (2 Tim. 4:5) by proclaiming the Word, not using manipulative techniques. You are to have that same commitment. When evangelizing the lost your main point is to proclaim "Jesus Christ and Him crucified" (1 Cor. 2:2). You are to tell the lost about the depravity of man, eternal judgment, the cross, the resurrection, the atonement, and Christ's second coming. As Spurgeon said, "Give the ungodly no rest in their sins" (*Lectures to My Students*, p. 345).

## VIII. THE GOAL OF THE PREACHER'S COMMISSION (v. 5d)

"Fulfill your ministry."

The Greek term translated "fulfill" (*plērophoreō*) means "to accomplish" and speaks of doing something wholeheartedly. Wholehearted ministry was certainly characteristic of Paul, who said, "I labor, striving according to His power, which mightily works within me" (Col. 1:29). It's no surprise that at the end of his life he could say, "I have finished the course" (2 Tim. 4:7). That reminds me of my grandfather. In the final days of his earthly life, he still had the desire to preach, wanting to fulfill all God had given him to do. Do you have a strong desire to finish your spiritual course? Endeavor to serve the Lord "with all your heart and with all your soul and with all your might" (Deut. 6:5).

## Focusing on the Facts

1. What makes the commands of 1 and 2 Timothy binding on all teachers (see p. 44)?
2. According to 2 Corinthians 5:20 what are you responsible to do (see p. 44)?
3. By exercising our _____ _____, each of us can serve Christ and His people (see p. 45).
4. According to Ephesians 4:11-12 why does God gift some men as pastors and teachers (see p. 46)?
5. Men who are called to preach are compelled to do so by the _____ _____ (see p. 47).
6. How does Scripture indicate Timothy's compulsion to preach (see pp. 47-48)?
7. How does God objectively shape a man's inner compulsion to preach (see pp. 48-49)?
8. According to 1 Timothy 3:2-7 what must the church evaluate? Why is that necessary (see pp. 49-50)?
9. What does 1 Thessalonians 2:1 reveal about the ministry of Paul and Timothy? How does that apply to the man who is pursuing the ministry today (see p. 50)?
10. What are two marks of an effective ministry (see p. 51)?
11. Why did Paul tell Timothy to be "a good soldier of Christ" (2 Tim. 2:3; see p. 51)?
12. According to Hebrews 13:23 how did Timothy suffer? What was the apparent cause of his suffering (see p. 51)?
13. What is the function of an evangelist (see p. 52)?
14. What are two important things to remember when proclaiming God's Word (see pp. 52-53)?
15. Why should you not manipulate people into a spiritual decision (see p. 53)?
16. How can you follow Paul's example and finish your spiritual course (Deut. 6:5; see pp. 53-54)?

## Pondering the Principles

1. The apostle Paul expressed his spiritual compulsion to share God's Word by saying, "Woe is me if I do not preach the gospel" (1 Cor. 9:16). Martyn Lloyd-Jones commented, "Is there any reason why Paul should be thus devoted, more than any other Christian? We cannot claim his gifts, and we have not received his special call to be an apostle, nor have we seen the risen Lord as he saw him. . . . But the same Lord has died for us, our debt to him is equally great. . . . Are we prepared to deny ourselves and to forego things

which are perfectly legitimate and lawful to us, for his sake and for the sake of those who know him not?. . . God grant that [your] response . . . may be a willing and entire surrender . . . to Christ and to his service" (*The Miracle of Grace* [Grand Rapids: Baker, 1986], pp. 59-60). Ponder those wise words and let them serve as a personal challenge.

2.  Like Timothy, you are to endure hardship in serving Christ. Look up the following verses and prayerfully meditate upon them, asking the Lord to help you endure all the trials you experience in life:

    • Job 23:11-12

    • Matthew 10:22

    • Galatians 6:9

    • Hebrews 12:1-3

    • James 1:2-4; 5:10-11

    • 1 Peter 2:19-21

# 5

# The Triumphant Epitaph of Paul—Part 1

## Outline

Introduction
A. The Meaning of Life
1. From an unbeliever's perspective
2. From a believer's perspective
B. The Ministry of Paul

Lesson
I.  Paul's Present Life (v. 6)
A. His Implicit Statement About Death (v. 6a)
1. Describing the sacrifice
a) Of a lamb
b) Of a larger animal
2. Identifying the worshiper
B. His Explicit Statement About Death (v. 6b)
1. The nearness of death
2. The pictures of death
a) Loosening an animal from its yoke
b) Loosening a prisoner from his chains
c) Loosening the ropes of a tent
d) Loosening the ropes of a ship
II. Paul's Past Life (v. 7)

## Introduction

A. The Meaning of Life

1. From an unbeliever's perspective

When you're near death, your final words will tend
to be stripped of any hypocrisy and reflect your view

of life. Near the end of his life, the notorious French statesman Talleyrand wrote, "Eighty-three years have passed! I am not sure I am pleased when I think back over how those years were spent. How many useless uproars there were; how many failures; how many outrageous complications; how much wasted emotion and energy, and how much wasted ability! Hatreds have been aroused, illusions lost, tastes jaded. And with what result? Moral and physical exhaustion, complete discouragement with respect to the future, deep disgust with repect to the past" (J. F. Bernard, *Talleyrand: A Biography* [N.Y.: G. P. Putnam's Sons, 1973], pp. 599-600).

2. From a believer's perspective

Paul's response to his imminent death is a stark contrast to that of a despairing unbeliever: "I am already being poured out as a drink offering, and the time of my departure has come. I have fought the good fight, I have finished the course, I have kept the faith; in the future there is laid up for me the crown of righteousness, which the Lord, the righteous Judge, will award to me on that day; and not only to me, but also to all who have loved His appearing" (2 Tim. 4:6-8). His words convey hope, joy, and victory, not despair or frustration.

B. The Ministry of Paul

Paul was a faithful shepherd of God's flock. His life was often in danger as he preached the gospel and nurtured the church. He was deeply concerned about the church's welfare. False teachers were teaching a false gospel, and some within the professing church were "paying attention to deceitful spirits and doctrines of demons" (1 Tim. 4:1). In addition, Paul was concerned about Timothy's spiritual life and therefore encouraged him to be courageous and faithful for the Lord.

Paul's ministry began more than thirty years ago on the Damascus Road (Acts 9:1-20). Now he was passing the baton of leadership to Timothy at a crucial time in the church's life. As Bible teacher William Barclay put it, "Paul, the aged warrior, is laying down his arms that Timothy may take them up" (*The Letters to Timothy, Titus, and Philemon*, rev. ed. [Philadelphia: Westminster, 1975], p. 208). I believe Paul was saying, "Timothy, because death is imminent for me, there's a compelling call for you to take my place and be a faithful leader. If you do that, you'll triumph at the end, just as I have."

Second Timothy 4:6-8 is Paul's final commentary, summary, and epitaph about his own life. In those verses he viewed his life from three perspectives:

- Verse 6 looks at the present—the close of Paul's life—and reveals his readiness.

- Verse 7 looks at the past—the course of Paul's life—and reveals his faithfulness.

- Verse 8 looks at the future—the crown of Paul's life—and reveals his reward.

Paul's final words aren't to be mistaken for pride, for he always credited God's power as enabling him to minister: e.g., "I labor, striving according to His power, which mightily works within me" (Col. 1:29). By God's grace he was faithful in serving the Lord, thus it was only appropriate to close his life with a triumphant epitaph. Let's look more closely at his final words, for they are a powerful motivator for us to serve Christ as faithfully as he did.

### Lesson

I. PAUL'S PRESENT LIFE (v. 6)

"For I am already being poured out as a drink offering, and the time of my departure has come."

A. His Implicit Statement About Death (v. 6a)

"For I am already being poured out as a drink offering."

"For I" in verse 6 introduces a contrast to "but you" in verse 5. Timothy was to be sober, endure hardship, do the work of an evangelist, and fulfill his ministry (v. 5) because Paul was about to die (v. 6).

Being a successor to such a godly leader put Timothy into a special group of Bible persons. That group includes Joshua, who succeeded Moses as the leader of Israel

(Josh. 1:1-2), and the prophet Elisha, the successor of Elijah (2 Kings 2:15).

"Already" (Gk., *ēdē*) refers to something that's now occurring, so the sense of 2 Timothy 4:6 is: "I am leaving or departing now." The word is used the same way of salvation in Romans 13:11, the mystery of iniquity in 2 Thessalonians 2:7, and the true light in 1 John 2:8. The Greek phrase translated "being poured out as a drink offering" (2 Tim. 4:6) is an allusion to an Old Testament sacrifice mentioned in Numbers 15.

In Numbers 15 the children of Israel were wandering in the desert under God's hand of judgment. The older generation eventually died there, but the Lord promised that the younger generation would enter the Promised Land. Since the new generation would continue to roam the desert for many years, God didn't want them to despair. So He taught them about the sacrifices they were to offer in their new territory. They served as a present reminder about their future homeland.

1. Describing the sacrifice

   *a)* Of a lamb

   This is what the Lord told Moses about the sacrifices: "When you enter the land where you are to live, which I am giving you, then make an offering by fire to the Lord, a burnt offering or a sacrifice to fulfill a special vow, or as a freewill offering or in your appointed times, to make a soothing aroma to the Lord, from the herd or from the flock.

   "And the one who presents his offering shall present to the Lord a grain offering of one-tenth of an ephah of fine flour mixed with one-fourth of a hin of oil, and you shall prepare wine for the libation, one-fourth of a hin, with the burnt offering or for the sacrifice, for each lamb" (Num. 15:1-5).

   A person would offer a lamb for a burnt offering, fine flour mixed in an oil base for a grain offering, and wine for a drink offering. The latter was to be poured out on the first two parts of the sacrifice. The conflagration of the sacrifice on the altar symbolized the worshiper's complete dedication to God (cf. Rom. 12:1).

*b*) Of a larger animal

For the sacrifice of a larger animal the grain and drink offerings were proportionately larger: "For a ram you shall prepare as a grain offering two-tenths of an ephah of fine flour mixed with one-third of a hin of oil; and for the libation you shall offer one-third of a hin of wine as a soothing aroma to the Lord.

"And when you prepare a bull as a burnt offering or a sacrifice, to fulfill a special vow, or for peace offerings to the Lord, then you shall offer with the bull a grain offering of three-tenths of an ephah of fine flour mixed with one-half a hin of oil; and you shall offer as the libation one-half a hin of wine as an offering by fire, as a soothing aroma to the Lord.

"Thus it shall be done for each ox, or for each ram, or for each of the male lambs, or of the goats. According to the number that you prepare, so you shall do for everyone according to their number" (Num. 15:6-12).

2. Identifying the worshiper

The Lord then identified who was allowed to offer the sacrifice: "All who are native shall do these things in this manner, in presenting an offering by fire, as a soothing aroma to the Lord. And if an alien sojourns with you, or one who may be among you throughout your generations, and he wishes to make an offering by fire, as a soothing aroma to the Lord, just as you do, so he shall do. As for the assembly, there shall be one statute for you and for the alien who sojourns with you, a perpetual statute throughout your generations; as you are, so shall the alien be before the Lord. There is to be one law and one ordinance for you and for the alien who sojourns with you" (vv. 13-16). Both Israelites and non-Israelites were permitted to offer a sacrifice to the Lord.

Of the three parts to the sacrifice, the drink offering was the capstone, for it was the final act of sacrifice.

Paul saw his entire ministry as an offering to the Lord, for he said, "[I am] a minister of Christ Jesus to the Gentiles, ministering as a priest the gospel of God, that my offering of the Gentiles might become acceptable, sanctified by the Holy Spirit" (Rom. 15:16). Perhaps he saw himself as the burnt offering, his ministry as the grain offering, and his death as the drink offering. Certainly the consummate act of his ministry, the final pouring out of his life, was literally fulfilled in his death: since Paul was a Roman citizen, his execution came by decapitation, not crucifixion.

This is what Paul said of the legal proceedings against him shortly before his death: "At my first defense no one supported me, but all deserted me; may it not be counted against them. But the Lord stood with me, and strengthened me, in order that through me the proclamation might be fully accomplished, and that all the Gentiles might hear; and I was delivered out of the lion's mouth. The Lord will deliver me from every evil deed, and will bring me safely to His heavenly kingdom; to Him be the glory forever and ever" (2 Tim. 4:16-18).

Although Paul was the spiritual father of many Gentile believers, no one supported him at his trial before King Nero. Now Paul was incarcerated in a dungeon, waiting to reappear before the king and receive his final sentence of death.

B. His Explicit Statement About Death (v. 6b)

"The time of my departure has come."

1. The nearness of death

The Greek term translated "time" (*kairos*) refers to a season rather than minutes, hours, or days. Paul sensed he had but a brief period of time before his actual death. That's why he told Timothy, "When you come bring the cloak which I left at Troas with Carpus, and the books, especially the parchments" (2 Tim. 4:13) and "make every effort to come before winter" (v. 21). Perhaps he sensed his death would occur in winter.

The perfect tense "has come" shows that the clouds of death were now hovering about him and would continue to do so until his execution. The apostle Peter obviously experienced that same sense of impending death, for he said, "The laying aside of my earthly dwelling is imminent" (2 Pet. 1:14).

## 2. The pictures of death

Instead of being terrified by death, Paul viewed it as a "departure" (Gk., *analusis*). His positive outlook reminds me of an African funeral custom. When a Christian dies, the people there say, "He's arrived," not "He's gone." Furthermore, Barclay noted four ways that *analusis* pictures death (*The Letters to Timothy, Titus, and Philemon*, p. 209):

*a)* Loosening an animal from its yoke

"It is the word for unyoking an animal from the shafts of the cart or the plough. Death to Paul was rest from toil." He would be glad to lay the burden down.

*b)* Loosening a prisoner from his chains

"It is the word for loosening bonds or fetters. Death for Paul was a release. He was to exchange the confines of a Roman prison for the glorious liberty of the courts of heaven." Death would release Paul from the bondage of indwelling sin and set him free to enjoy the glorious liberty of righteousness.

*c)* Loosening the ropes of a tent

"It is the word for loosening the ropes of a tent. For Paul it was time to strike camp again. Many a journey he made across the roads of Asia Minor and of Europe. Now he was setting out on his last and greatest journey; he was taking the road that led to God." Paul was a tentmaker by trade (Acts 18:3), so he knew how to pull up stakes and break camp. Soon his own bodily tent would be taken down that he might embark on a heavenly journey.

*d)* To loose the ropes from a ship

"It is the word for loosening the mooring-ropes of a ship. Many a time Paul had felt his ship leave the harbour for the deep waters. Now he is to launch out into the greatest deep of all, setting sail to cross the waters of death to arrive in the haven of eternity." You secure a ship in its harbor by tying it to sturdy poles with rope. When it's time for the ship to leave harbor, the ropes are released. The ropes of Paul's earthly life would soon be let loose that he might set sail for the harbor of heaven.

For us as Christians, death lays down our yoke of sin that we might receive our heavenly rest. Death lays aside our shackle of sin that we might be free from its presence. Death takes down our earthly tent that we might take up our heavenly residence. Death casts off our ropes of sin that we might set sail for heaven. Those pictorial truths give us all the more reason not to fear death (cf. 1 Cor. 15:55-57).

I believe Paul faced death the same way Christ did. Jesus said, "No one has taken [My life] away from Me, but I lay it down on My own initiative" (John 10:18). As for Paul, he didn't avoid death by denying the faith or compromising his situation. He didn't become frustrated and ask, "How can this happen?" Rather, he willingly took up his cross by following Christ even to the point of death (cf. Matt. 16:24).

## Dying with True Dignity

Paul considered it a privilege and honor not only to suffer for Christ, but also to die for Him. His attitude reminds me of Robert Browning's "Incident of the French Camp." Browning's poem tells of a young soldier who hurriedly came from the battlefield to report victory to the French emperor Napoleon. He was so exhilarated to report the good news and so honored to be chosen as the messenger that he was oblivious to his own severe wounds. Napoleon, upon noting them, exclaimed:

"You're wounded!" "Nay," the soldier's pride
Touched to the quick, he said:
"I'm killed, Sire!" And his chief beside,
Smiling the boy fell dead.

Paul spoke of the wounds he received in serving Christ: "I bear on my body the brand-marks of Jesus" (Gal. 6:17). Those wounds were a testimony of Paul's willingness to accept even death for the cause of Christ. What about you? Are you willing to accept wounds or even death to serve as Christ would have you?

## II.  PAUL'S PAST LIFE (v. 7)

"I have fought the good fight, I have finished the course, I have kept the faith."

This is a flashback of Paul's life. In the Greek text that is emphasized in two ways. First, the object of the sentence comes before the verb: "The good fight I have fought, the course I have finished, the faith I have kept." Second, the perfect tense of the verbs speaks of actions completed in the past with results continuing into the present.

Paul looked back on his life without any sense of regret, sadness, or unfulfillment. Let's learn from his triumphant epitaph that we might do the same!

### Focusing on the Facts

1. What do Paul's final words convey in 2 Timothy 4:6-8 (see p. 58)?
2. Paul was a _____ shepherd of God's flock. Approximately how long did he minister (see p. 58)?
3. What were two of Paul's concerns about the church (see p. 58)?
4. What three perspectives does 2 Timothy 4:6-8 represent (see p. 59)?
5. Why aren't Paul's final words to be mistaken for pride (Col. 1:29; see p. 59)?
6. What is the significance of the phrase translated "for I" in 2 Timothy 4:6 (see p. 59)?
7. In what way is Timothy like Joshua and Elisha (see p. 59)?
8. Summarize how Numbers 15 relates to Paul's "drink offering" in 2 Timothy 4:6 (see pp. 60-61).
9. How was Paul strengthened while facing imminent death (2 Tim. 4:16-18; see p. 62)?
10. What is the meaning of "time" in 2 Timothy 4:6 (see p. 62).
11. What is the significance of "has come" in 2 Timothy 4:6 (see p. 62)?
12. What are four ways that *analusis* pictures death? How do those pictures apply to you as a Christian (see pp. 63-64)?
13. In what sense did Paul face death like Christ (see p. 64)?
14. What were Paul's wounds a testimony of (see p. 64)?
15. Second Timothy 4:7 is a _____ of Paul's life (see p. 65).
16. In what sense did Paul look back on his life (see p. 65)?

# Pondering the Principles

1. Paul was willing to suffer and die to serve Christ. His attitude is reminiscent of Henry Lyte's hymn "Jesus, I My Cross Have Taken":

   > Jesus, I my cross have taken, all to leave and follow Thee;
   > Destitute, despised, forsaken, Thou, from hence, my all shalt be:
   > Perish every fond ambition, all I've sought, and hoped, and known;
   > Yet how rich is my condition, God and heaven are still my own!
   >
   > Haste thee on from grace to glory, armed by faith and winged by prayer;
   > Heaven's eternal day's before thee, God's own hand shall guide thee there.
   > Soon shall close thy earthly mission, swift shall pass thy pilgrim days,
   > Hope shall change to glad fruition, faith to sight, and prayer to praise.

   With that in mind, read and meditate on 2 Corinthians 5:1-9. Commune with God over the truths in that passage.

2. In his book *Dying Thoughts* the Puritan Richard Baxter, a preacher for over forty years, wrote, "Many serious Christians, through the weakness of their trust in God, live in this perplexed strait, weary of living and afraid of dying, continually pressed between grief and fear. But Paul's strait was between two joys, which of them he should desire most. And if that be my case, what should much interrupt my peace or pleasure? If I live, it is for Christ, for his service. . . . If I die presently, it is my gain; God, who appoints me my work, limits my time; and surely his glorious reward can never be unseasonable, or come too soon, if it be the time that he appoints" ([Grand Rapids: Baker, 1976], pp. 19-20). Can you say with Paul, "To live is Christ, and to die is gain" (Phil. 1:21)? Ask the Lord to help you have a biblical attitude toward life and death.

# 6

# The Triumphant Epitaph of Paul—Part 2

### Outline

Introduction

Review
I.   Paul's Present Life (v. 6)
II.  Paul's Past Life (v. 7)

Lesson
A. He Recognized the Spiritual Struggle (v. 7a)
B. He Recognized the Nobility of the Cause (v. 7a)
C. He Recognized the Need to Stay on Course (v. 7b)
D. He Recognized the Need to Treasure Time (v. 7b)
E. He Recognized the Fulfillment of a Sacred Trust (v. 7c)

### Introduction

Years ago President Theodore Roosevelt gave this penetrating call to commitment: "It's not the critic who counts; not the man who points out how the strong man stumbled or where the doer of deeds could have done better. The credit belongs to the man who is actually in the arena, whose face is marred by dust and sweat and blood, who strives valiantly; who errs, and comes short again and again, because there is no effort without error and shortcoming; who does actually try to do the deed; who knows the great enthusiasm, the great devotion and spends himself in a worthy cause; who, at the worst, if he fails, at least fails while daring greatly. Far better is it to dare mighty things, to win glorious triumphs even though checked by failure, than to rank with those poor spirits who neither enjoy nor suffer much because they live in a gray twilight that knows neither victory nor defeat" (cf. Hamilton Club speech on the strenuous life, Chicago, 10 Apr. 1899).

Certainly the apostle Paul didn't live in a gray twilight, for his life reflected great commitment and courage as he ministered triumphantly on behalf of Christ. Now he was calling Timothy to follow in his steps.

Second Timothy 4:6-8 is Paul's final summary of his Christian life. He was now in prison and knew death was imminent. Yet his attitude was not one of fear or regret, but of triumph. And I believe his longing was for all Christians to have a triumphant epitaph.

## Review

I.  PAUL'S PRESENT LIFE (v. 6; see pp. 59-64)

   A.  His Implicit Statement About Death (v. 6a; see pp. 59-62)

   B.  His Explicit Statement About Death (v. 6b; see pp. 62-64)

II.  PAUL'S PAST LIFE (v. 7; see p. 65)

   "I have fought the good fight, I have finished the course, I have kept the faith."

## Lesson

That verse is a flashback that summarizes Paul's ministry and reveals his faithfulness to the Lord. The perfect-tense verbs show that he fought the good fight, continued the course, and kept the faith all along the way. He looked back on his life without any sense of unfulfillment because he knew he accomplished all that God had called and equipped him to do. We can do the same by following Paul's example in verse 7. Five principles stand out.

A.  He Recognized the Spiritual Struggle (v. 7a)

   "I have fought the good *fight*."

   The Greek term translated "fought" (*agonizomai*, from which we derive *agony*) refers to a struggle. It pictures a contest requiring the expenditure of great effort or energy. The Bible uses the analogies of a track meet (1 Cor. 9:24), a boxing match (v. 26), and a wrestling contest (Eph. 6:12) to describe such an effort. To be victorious, a believer must recognize that he or she is engaged in a spiritual struggle.

Bible scholar William Hendricksen described Paul's spiritual struggle like this: "It had been a fight against Satan; against the principalities and powers, the world-rulers of this darkness in the heavenlies; against Jewish and pagan vice and violence; against Judaism among the Galatians; against fanaticism among the Thessalonians; against contention, fornication, and litigation among the Corinthians; against incipient Gnosticism among the Ephesians and Colossians; against fightings without and fears within; and last but not least, against the law of sin and death operating within his own heart" (*Exposition of Thessalonians, Timothy and Titus* [Grand Rapids: Baker, 1957], p. 315).

All Christians are engaged in spiritual warfare that requires maximum effort and commitment. Anything less reflects an apathetic attitude toward the cause of Christ. Paul labored to the point of exhaustion (Col. 1:29) and said believers will suffer on Christ's behalf (Phil 1:29-30). Serving the Lord requires labor and effort, not part-time indulgence.

B. He Recognized the Nobility of the Cause (v. 7a)

"I have fought the *good* fight."

"Good" (Gk., *kalos*) can be translated "beautiful," "useful," or "excellent," but my favorite translation is "noble." For Paul the noblest cause was serving Christ. However, that's not true for all believers since many "seek after their own interests, not those of Christ Jesus" (Phil. 2:21).

Paul was so consumed with advancing Christ's kingdom that he said, "Whatever things were gain to me, those things I have counted as loss for the sake of Christ. More than that, I count all things to be loss in view of the surpassing value of knowing Christ Jesus my Lord, for whom I have suffered the loss of all things, and count them but rubbish in order that I may gain Christ" (Phil. 3:7-8).

Rather than rest on his impressive earthly credentials, Paul forsook all to follow Christ. Timothy did the same, for Paul said, "He is doing the Lord's work, as I also am" (1 Cor. 16:10).

God calls all believers to the noble cause of serving as "ambassadors for Christ" (2 Cor. 5:20). Since ours is a heavenly and holy calling, we should never rest or let our guard down while engaged in the spiritual struggle. Instead we are to run the race with courage. And it has been well said that courage is fear that has said its prayers.

Examine your own life and ask, *Am I truly serving Christ? How has God gifted and equipped me? Am I devoting my time, energy, and talents for the cause of Christ or have I been wasting my life on trivial things?*

## C. He Recognized the Need to Stay on Course (v. 7*b*)

"I have finished *the course.*"

Although many believers start out on the right course, they eventually become diverted from the track God originally set them on. The race begins when a believer is born into God's kingdom, and ends when he enters God's presence. The interval between is the time he has to complete his spiritual course. If he strays from his course he loses valuable time. The only way to complete the course within the allotted time is to stay on course.

The Greek term translated "course" (*dromos*) pictures an athletic race (cf. Acts 20:24; 1 Cor. 9:27). In running his spiritual race the believer is to "lay aside every encumbrance" (Heb. 12:1), which refers to any unnecessary weight or baggage. When competing in a race, a runner doesn't wear an overcoat or carry luggage. Similarly, the believer is to discard anything that impedes him from doing his best and finishing his course. That obviously includes sin, but could also include things that are not.

Our toughest battle in the Christian life is to stay on course, and that requires self-discipline. Such discipline was manifested by the early church. In Acts 6 the twelve apostles said, "It is not desirable for us to neglect the word of God in order to serve tables. . . . But we will devote ourselves to prayer, and to the ministry of the word" (vv. 2, 4). Paul said, "I do not consider my life of any account as dear to myself, in order that I may finish my course, and the ministry which I received from the

Lord Jesus, to testify solemnly of the gospel of the grace of God" (Acts 20:24).

Since Christ is the perfect example of One who stayed on course, we are to fix "our eyes on Jesus, the author and perfecter of faith" (Heb. 12:2). Christ was always mindful of doing His Father's will: "I have come down from heaven, not to do My own will, but the will of Him who sent Me" (John 6:38). We should follow Christ because He is perfect in holiness and "without sin" (Heb. 4:15).

Focusing on our spiritual course can be a difficult thing to do. Peter, for example, became distracted over God's plan for the apostle John (John 21:18-23). And I believe many Christians are distracted from what God has called and gifted them to do. They want to run their own course because they fear the self-discipline that God's course requires.

## The Essence of Self-Discipline

I believe Rudyard Kipling's "If—" expresses the essence of a disciplined life:

> If you can keep your head when all about you
>     Are losing theirs and blaming it on you,
> If you can trust yourself when all men doubt you,
>     But make allowance for their doubting too,
> If you can wait and not be tired by waiting,
>     Or being lied about, don't deal in lies,
> Or being hated, don't give way to hating,
>     And yet don't look too good, nor talk too wise:
>
> If you can dream—and not make dreams your master;
>     If you can think—and not make thoughts your aim;
> If you can meet with Triumph and Disaster
>     And treat those two impostors just the same.
>
> If you can make one heap of all your winnings
>     And risk it on one turn of pitch-and-toss,
> And lose, and start again at your beginnings
>     And never breathe a word about your loss.
>
> If you can talk with crowds and keep your virtue,
>     Or walk with kings—nor lose the common touch,
> If neither foes nor loving friends can hurt you,
>     If all men count with you, but none too much;

If you can fill the unforgiving minute
    With sixty seconds' worth of distance run,
Yours is the Earth and everything that's in it,
    And—which is more—you'll be a Man, my son!

Exercise self-discipline and run God's course!

## The Baseball Focus

Ted Williams was a great baseball player. When he was ready to hit the ball, it was said that players sometimes threw fire-crackers at his feet to distract him. But because of his tremendous ability to concentrate and focus on the ball he didn't even hear them go off. Similarly, in the spiritual realm we must have a biblical focus to stay on course.

D. He Recognized the Need to Treasure Time (v. 7*b*)

"I have *finished* the course."

As a believer you have a limited time to finish your spiritual race. In a sense you are running against the clock just like at a track meet. So make "the most of your time, because the days are evil" (Eph. 5:16). We must see time for what it truly is: a treasure God gives us.

Paul finished his course because he used his time wisely. William Barclay gave this illustration: "The Battle of Marathon was one of the decisive battles of the world. In it the Greeks met the Persians, and, if the Persians had conquered, the glory that was Greece would never have flowered upon the world. Against fearful odds the Greeks won the victory, and, after the battle, a Greek soldier ran all the way, day and night, to Athens with the news. Straight to the magistrates he ran. 'Rejoice,' he gasped, 'we have conquered,' and even as he delivered his message he fell dead. He had completed his course and done his work, and there is no finer way for any man to die" (*The Letters to Timothy, Titus, and Philemon*, rev. ed. [Philadelphia: Westminster, 1975], pp. 210-11).

Today's marathon race is a tribute to that faithful soldier. Its distance is supposed to be the same as what he ran. As Christians we are to make the most of our time in delivering God's divine message (cf. Rom. 10:14).

Our responsibility to treasure time reminds me of what my track coach said years ago: "If you have anything left ten yards past the finish line, you didn't give your all." Realizing our time is so short, we should give no less than our best to the Lord.

## E. He Recognized the Fulfillment of a Sacred Trust (v. 7c)

"I have kept the faith."

Paul recognized he was fulfilling a sacred trust—God's Word. It was the controlling element in everything he did, and should be for us as well. We are to fight the good fight, realize the nobility of the cause, run with self-discipline, finish our spiritual race, and value time as a treasure because God's Word tells us to.

In verse 7 "the faith" refers to the revealed Word of God, and "I have kept" (Gk., tēreō) means "to guard." We are to run the race obeying and proclaiming God's Word, but never compromising its truth. That's why Paul told Timothy, "Guard what has been entrusted to you, avoiding worldly and empty chatter and the opposing arguments of what is falsely called 'knowledge' " (1 Tim. 6:20) and through the Holy Spirit who dwells in us "guard . . . the treasure which has been entrusted to you" (2 Tim. 1:14).

As Christians we are to "contend earnestly for the faith which was once for all delivered to the saints" (Jude 1:3). We are to guard God's Word even in the midst of hostile opposition because it's the treasure of all treasures.

## The Little Blind Girl Who Loved God's Word

A missionary in France told of a little French girl who became a believer. Although she had been blind from birth, she knew how to read Braille. Someone gave her the gospel of Mark in Braille, and she loved it so much that she eventually developed calluses on her fingers from reading it so often. Those calluses meant she no longer could read.

Hoping to make her fingers more sensitive, she peeled the skin from the end of her fingers. But instead her fingers became permanently scarred. Believing she would never read again, she bent down to give the pages of God's Word a farewell kiss. As she did, she soon realized that her lips were more sensitive than her fingers. She then learned how to read God's Word with her lips.

Do you desire to have a love for the Word like that? Your Christian life is a direct reflection of how you view the treasure of God's Word.

## Focusing on the Facts

1. What did the life of the apostle Paul reflect (see p. 68)?
2. Why didn't Paul have any sense of unfulfillment (see p. 68)?
3. What does "fought" refer to in 2 Timothy 4:7 (see p. 69)?
4. Describe Paul's spiritual struggle (see p. 69).
5. Spiritual warfare requires maximum _____ and _____ (see p. 69).
6. What does Philippians 1:29-30 teach (see p. 69)?
7. What was the noblest cause for Paul? Why isn't that true for all believers (Phil. 2:21; see p. 69)?
8. God calls all believers to the noble cause of serving as "____ ___ for Christ" (2 Cor. 5:20; see p. 70).
9. Because your calling is heavenly and holy, what should you never do (see p. 70)?
10. What is the only way to complete your course (see p. 70)?
11. According to Hebrews 12:1 what is the believer to lay aside? Why (see p. 70)?
12. In what way did the apostles manifest self-discipline (Acts 6:2, 4; 20:24; see pp. 70-71)?
13. What was Christ always mindful of (John 6:38; see p. 71)?
14. Why do many believers want to run their own course instead of God's (see p. 71)?
15. What does Ephesians 5:16 teach (see p. 72)?
16. What is to be the controlling element in everything we do (see p. 73)?

## Pondering the Principles

1. Hebrews 12:1-2 says, "Let us run with endurance the race that is set before us, fixing our eyes on Jesus, the author and perfecter of faith." Martyn Lloyd-Jones said, "We cannot change circumstances, but we can triumph in them. We can be 'more than conquerors'; and we become so as we are found 'looking unto Jesus.' Look at Him! Look at the nights He spent in prayer, look at His knowledge of the Word of God, look at the way in which He 'exercised His senses.' . . .

We must become imitators of Him. We must look beyond men, we must look to the Son of God and what He has done in order 'to save us out of this present evil world,' and to introduce us to the glory that awaits us with God" (*The Christian Soldier* [Grand Rapids: Baker, 1977], pp. 93-94). Stay on course and finish your spiritual race by looking to Christ.

2. You are to fight "the *good* fight" (2 Tim. 4:7, emphasis added). Take comfort from these words of English minister J. C. Ryle, who explains why it is good: "Let us settle it in our minds that the Christian fight is a good fight—really good, truly good, emphatically good. We see only part of it yet. We see the struggle, but not the end; we see the campaign, but not the reward; we see the cross, but not the crown. We see a few humble, broken-spirited, penitent, praying people, enduring hardships and despised by the world; but we see not the hand of God over them, the face of God smiling on them, the kingdom of glory prepared for them. These things are yet to be revealed. Let us not judge by appearances. There are more good things about the Christian warfare than we see" (*Holiness* [Hertfordshire, Eng.: Evangelical Press, 1989], p. 62).

# 7
# The Triumphant Epitaph of Paul—Part 3

## Outline

Introduction

Review
I.   Paul's Present Life (v. 6)
II.  Paul's Past Life (v. 7)

Lesson
III. Paul's Future Life (v. 8)
   A. The Anticipation of His Reward
   B. The Honor of His Reward
   C. The Meaning of His Reward
   D. The Descriptions of His Reward
   E. The Reasons for His Reward
      1. His service to Christ
      2. His faithfulness to Christ
   F. The Reception of His Reward
      1. The time
      2. The people

## Introduction

God's people are the recipients of His abundant grace. The culmination of that grace is His plan to reward those who love Him. That plan is mentioned throughout Scripture.

A. Genesis 15:1—God said to Abraham, "Your reward shall be very great."

B. Luke 6:22-23—Christ said, "Blessed are you when men hate you, and ostracize you, and cast insults at you, and spurn your name as evil, for the sake of the Son of Man. Be glad in that day, and leap for joy, for behold, your reward is great in heaven." Although believers must endure persecution in this life, God has prepared a great reward for them in heaven.

C. 1 Corinthians 2:9—God has prepared "things which eye has not seen and ear has not heard, and which have not entered the heart of man" for those who love Him (cf. Isa. 64:4).

D. Ephesians 2:4-7—"God, being rich in mercy, because of His great love with which He loved us, even when we were dead in our transgressions, made us alive together with Christ (by grace you have been saved), and raised us up with Him, and seated us with Him in the heavenly places, in Christ Jesus, in order that in the ages to come He might show the surpassing riches of His grace in kindness toward us in Christ Jesus."

E. 1 Peter 1:3-5—"Blessed be the God and Father of our Lord Jesus Christ, who according to His great mercy has caused us to be born again to a living hope through the resurrection of Jesus Christ from the dead, to obtain an inheritance which is imperishable and undefiled and will not fade away, reserved in heaven for you, who are protected by the power of God through faith for a salvation ready to be revealed in the last time."

F. Psalm 58:11—"Surely there is a reward for the righteous."

G. Hebrews 11:6—God "is a rewarder of those who seek Him."

H. Philippians 3:8, 14—Paul said, "I count all things to be loss in view of the surpassing value of knowing Christ Jesus my Lord, for whom I have suffered the loss of all things, and count them but rubbish in order that I may gain Christ. . . . I press on toward the goal for the prize of the upward call of God in Christ Jesus." Paul lived in light of his eternal reward.

I. Romans 8:18—Paul said, "I consider that the sufferings of this present time are not worthy to be compared with the glory that is to be revealed to us."

J. 2 Corinthians 4:17-18—Paul also said that our "momentary, light affliction is producing for us an eternal weight of glory far beyond all comparison, while we look not at the things which are seen, but at the things which are not seen; for the things which are seen are temporal, but the things which are not seen are eternal." He eagerly anticipated his eternal glory in heaven.

Second Timothy 4:8 is another place where we see Paul looking toward his future reward.

## Review

I. PAUL'S PRESENT LIFE (v. 6; see pp. 59-64)

A. His Implicit Statement About Death (v. 6a; see pp. 59-62)

B. His Explicit Statement About Death (v. 6b; see pp. 62-64)

II. PAUL'S PAST LIFE (v. 7; see pp. 68-74)

A. He Recognized the Spiritual Struggle (v. 7a; see pp. 68-69)

B. He Recognized the Nobility of the Cause (v. 7a; see pp. 69-70)

C. He Recognized the Need to Stay on Course (v. 7b; see pp. 70-72)

D. He Recognized the Need to Treasure Time (v. 7b; see pp. 72-73)

E. He Recognized the Fulfillment of a Sacred Trust (v. 7c; see pp. 73-74)

## Lesson

III. PAUL'S FUTURE LIFE (v. 8)

"In the future there is laid up for me the crown of righteousness, which the Lord, the righteous Judge, will award to me on that day; and not only to me, but also to all who have loved His appearing."

## A. The Anticipation of His Reward

"In the future" is when Paul would receive his reward. When an athlete wins a fight or race, he looks forward to his trophy or reward. Similarly, Paul anticipated the eternal reward he would receive for finishing his spiritual race. The Greek verb translated "laid up" (*apokeimai*) speaks of safely storing away or depositing something. The crown or wreath pictures an athletic award. Paul knew his reward was safely deposited in heaven (cf. 1 Tim. 6:19).

## B. The Honor of His Reward

The Greek term translated "crown" (*stephanos*) refers to a wreath that was usually woven like a garland and placed on someone's head. In Matthew 27:29 it describes the crown of thorns placed on Christ's head. Back then a *stephanos* was worn for various reasons: it was worn by retiring civil magistrates in honor of their faithful service, it was worn at festivals as a sign of celebration and joy, and it was worn at pagan temples to honor the gods.

The most well known use of a *stephanos* was to reward an athlete for his victory in a contest. Paul used that analogy in 2 Timothy 2:5: "If anyone competes as an athlete, he does not win the prize unless he competes according to the rules." An athlete's wreath is perishable, but the one Christ will honor believers with is imperishable (1 Pet. 1:4).

## C. The Meaning of His Reward

Paul described the crown he would receive as "the crown of righteousness" (2 Tim. 4:8). Some believe a righteous life is the basis of the reward. That interpretation is possible linguistically, but it contradicts what we know of Paul's humility.

I believe the crown is righteousness itself. The believer is considered righteous when he or she comes to Christ (Rom. 5:21). Righteousness is also a practical part of Christian growth since we were freed from sin to become "slaves of righteousness" (Rom. 6:18). But I believe the righteousness in 2 Timothy 4:8 refers to the perfect and eternal righteousness of heaven. God's Word speaks of it this way:

1. Romans 14:17—"The kingdom of God is not eating and drinking, but righteousness and peace and joy in the Holy Spirit."

2. Galatians 5:5—"We through the Spirit, by faith, are waiting for the hope of righteousness." Every true believer longs for perfect and eternal righteousness.

3. 2 Peter 3:13—"We are looking for new heavens and a new earth, in which righteousness dwells." In heaven there will be no sin (cf. Rev. 21:8, 27).

4. James 1:12—"Blessed is a man who perseveres under trial; for once he has been approved, he will receive the crown of life, which the Lord has promised to those who love Him." The crown of life is like the crown of righteousness, and all who love Christ will receive it.

5. 1 Peter 5:4—"When the Chief Shepherd appears, you will receive the unfading crown of glory." The crown of glory is like the crown of righteousness and is also promised to every believer.

Christ will reward all believers in heaven with eternal righteousness, life, and glory. Such righteousness means the absence of sin, defeat, and death. Paul's greatest battle came not from false teachers or Satan, but his own sinful nature (Rom. 7:5-25). He was weary from fighting his own fallenness and longed for absolute and perfect righteousness.

D. The Descriptions of His Reward

God's Word describes the perfect righteousness of heaven as: being with Christ (Phil. 1:23), seeing God (Matt. 5:8), beholding the glory of Christ (John 17:24), being glorified with Christ (Rom. 8:17), reigning with Christ forever (2 Tim. 2:12; Rev. 22:5), being joint heirs with Christ (Rom. 8:17), inheriting all things (Col. 1:12; Rev. 21:7), shining as the stars (Dan. 12:3), enjoying everlasting light (Isa. 60:19), entering the joy of the Lord (Matt. 25:21), enjoying eternal rest (Heb. 4:9), entering the fullness of joy (Ps. 16:11), receiving the prize of our high calling (Phil. 3:14), possessing treasure in heaven (Matt. 19:21), and benefiting from an eternal weight of glory (2 Cor. 4:17).

## E. The Reasons for His Reward

The parable of the laborers in the vineyard (Matt. 20:1-16) shows that all believers receive the reward of eternal righteousness. Some of the laborers worked many hours, but others worked just one hour. At the end of the day the landowner paid all the laborers the same wage. No matter what our service is, how long we work, or how hard we work, in the end we all receive the same "wage" of eternal life and righteousness.

Although 2 Timothy 4:8 refers to the general reward of perfect righteousness for all believers in heaven, God's Word also speaks about additional rewards we receive for our service and faithfulness to Christ.

1. His service to Christ

   *a)* Romans 14:10-12—"We shall all stand before the judgment seat of God. For it is written, 'As I live, says the Lord, every knee shall bow to Me, and every tongue shall give praise to God' [Isa. 45:23]. So then each one of us shall give account of himself to God." God will evaluate our service to Him and reward us accordingly.

   *b)* 2 Corinthians 5:10—"We must all appear before the judgment seat of Christ, that each one may be recompensed for his deeds in the body, according to what he has done, whether good or bad." The Greek term translated "bad" (*phaulos*) refers to something that is worthless, not sinful. Judgment of our sins is not in view here, for there is "no condemnation for those who are in Christ Jesus" (Rom. 8:1). Christ has put away our sins forever. Nevertheless, Christ will evaluate our ministry to see what was valuable or worthless.

   *c)* 1 Corinthians 3:12-15—"If any man builds upon the foundation with gold, silver, precious stones, wood, hay, straw, each man's work will become evident; for the day will show it, because it is to be revealed with fire; and the fire itself will test the quality of each man's work. If any man's work which he has built upon it remains, he shall receive a reward. If any man's work is burned up, he shall suffer loss; but he himself shall be saved, yet so as through fire."

Wood, hay, and straw represent that which is meaningless spiritually, while gold, silver, and precious stones represent what is truly useful in the advancement of God's kingdom. The worth of our service will become evident at the judgment seat of Christ. Wood, hay, and straw will burn up, but gold, silver, and precious stones will remain. Whatever remains will be the basis of our special reward, but whatever burns up will be forever lost to us.

I believe these special rewards relate to the capacity and nature of our eternal service. We all will have the crown of eternal righteousness, but each of us will do different things (cf. Rev. 22:3).

2.  His faithfulness to Christ

Scripture teaches that the sphere and nature of our service, authority, and co-regency with Christ throughout eternity is determined by the faithfulness of our service here on earth.

*a*)  Matthew 25:14-30—The person who was faithful in managing a few talents was entrusted with managing even more. Similarly, if we are faithful in serving the Lord here, we will receive greater responsibility in eternity.

*b*)  Luke 12:42-44—Christ said, "Who then is the faithful and sensible steward, whom his master will put in charge of his servants, to give them their rations at the proper time? Blessed is that slave whom his master finds so doing when he comes. Truly I say to you, that he will put him in charge of all his possessions." If we are faithful in ministry, our authority and responsibilities will be greater when He returns.

*c*)  2 John 1:8—"Watch yourselves, that you might not lose what we have accomplished, but that you may receive a full reward." The greatest joy for the believer both here and in eternity is to serve Christ. How we serve Christ now is vital: it determines our capacity to serve Him in heaven.

*d*)  Revelation 3:11—Christ said, "I am coming quickly; hold fast what you have, in order that no one take your crown." We are to be faithful and not lose our reward because of sin.

*e)* Revelation 2:26—Christ also said, "He who overcomes, and he who keeps My deeds until the end, to him I will give authority over the nations." He who obeys Christ will reign with Him.

*f)* Luke 19:11-27—Since his servants managed his money wisely, a nobleman gave them authority over cities. Similarly, our authority in heaven is directly proportional to how well we make use of the gifts God has given us in advancing His kingdom.

F. The Reception of His Reward

Paul longed to receive his crown of eternal righteousness from "the Lord, the righteous Judge" (2 Tim. 4:8; cf. v. 1). Christ knows the value or inferiority of our service because His judgment is perfect. Christ will "award" (Gk., *apodidōmi*) or recompense us with the general reward of eternal righteousness and Christlikeness, and any specific reward for our faithful service.

1. The time

We will receive our rewards "on that day" (2 Tim. 4:8; cf. 1:12, 18), a reference to the Judgment Seat of Christ. I believe that will occur in heaven right after the rapture of the church. Before that time believers have eternal righteousness, life, and glory, but not in its fullness. That's because their bodies have not yet been glorified. While those in heaven are already serving and reigning with Christ in some way, the fullest and final expression of it awaits the Lord's return for His church. At that time Christ will settle His accounts and reward His faithful servants.

*a)* 1 Corinthians 4:5—"Do not go on passing judgment before the time, but wait until the Lord comes who will both bring to light the things hidden in the darkness and disclose the motives of men's hearts; and then each man's praise will come to him from God."

*b)* Revelation 22:12—Christ said, "Behold, I am coming quickly, and My reward is with Me."

*c)* 1 Thessalonians 4:16-17—"The Lord Himself will descend from heaven with a shout, with the voice of the archangel, and with the trumpet of God; and the dead in Christ shall rise first. We who are alive and remain shall be caught up together with them in the clouds to meet the Lord in the air, and thus we shall always be with the Lord."

*d)* Luke 14:14—Christ said, "You will be repaid at the resurrection of the righteous." When our bodies are resurrected and glorified, we will express eternal righteousness in its fullness.

*e)* 1 Thessalonians 2:19—Paul asked, "Who is our hope or joy or crown of exultation? Is it not even you, in the presence of our Lord Jesus at His coming?" The crown of Paul's ministry and the supreme joy of his life was knowing he would see believers he had nurtured present at Christ's return. That's when both soul and body will join in fully expressing eternal righteousness and Christlikeness.

2. The people

The reward of eternal righteousness is for Paul and "all who have loved His appearing" (2 Tim. 4:8). The verb's perfect tense speaks of a continual love, thus "all" refers to all believers. The greatest mark of a true believer is his or her love for God.

*a)* John 5:42—Christ characterized unbelievers this way: "You do not have the love of God in yourselves."

*b)* John 14:21, 23—Christ said, "He who has My commandments and keeps them, he it is who loves Me; and he who loves Me shall be loved by My Father, and I will love him, and will disclose Myself to him. . . . If anyone loves Me, he will keep My word; and My Father will love him, and We will come to him, and make Our abode with him." In regeneration God enables us to love Him.

*c)* Romans 5:5—"The love of God has been poured out within our hearts through the Holy Spirit who was given to us."

*d)* 1 John 4:7—"Everyone who loves is born of God and knows God."

*e)* Philippians 3:20—Paul said, "Our citizenship is in heaven, from which also we eagerly wait for a Savior, the Lord Jesus Christ." Because we love Christ, we eagerly look for His return.

*f)* 1 Corinthians 16:22—"If anyone does not love the Lord, let him be accursed." Only believers love the Lord.

Do you love Christ? Do you show it by delighting in and obeying God's Word? If so, you'll receive an eternal reward of perfect righteousness in eternity. You can enhance and enrich that eternal reward by faithfully serving Christ now. That's why Paul said, "Whatever you do, do your work heartily, as for the Lord rather than for men; knowing that from the Lord you will receive the reward of the inheritance. It is the Lord Christ whom you serve" (Col. 3:23-24). By loving and serving Christ with all your heart, you'll enjoy eternity as Christ expresses back to you His gratitude for your service. He will do so by enhancing your service and responsibility beyond what you can imagine! You'll know the fullness of eternal joy as you serve the One who gave Himself for you.

### Focusing on the Facts

1. What is the culmination of God's grace (see p. 78)?
2. How does 1 Peter 1:4 describe our inheritance (see p. 78)?
3. What is our "momentary, light affliction" producing (2 Cor. 4:17; see p. 79)?
4. What is Paul looking toward in 2 Timothy 4:8 (see p. 79)?
5. What does "laid up" mean in verse 8? How does that apply to our eternal reward (see p. 80)?
6. What does "the crown of righteousness" refer to in verse 8 (see p. 80-81)?
7. How does God's Word describe our reward (see p. 81-82)?
8. What is not in view at the Judgment Seat of Christ? Why (Rom. 8:1; see p. 82)?
9. What does 1 Corinthians 3:12-15 teach (see pp. 82-83)?
10. What do our special rewards relate to (see p. 83)?
11. What does Matthew 25:14-30 teach (see p. 83)?

12. When will we receive our reward of righteousness (see pp. 84-85)?
13. What was the supreme joy of Paul's life? Why (see p. 85)?
14. Whom does "all" refer to in 2 Timothy 4:8 (see p. 85)?
15. What is the greatest mark of a true believer? Support your answer with Scripture (see pp. 85-86).
16. How can you enhance and enrich your eternal reward (Col. 3:23-24; see p. 86)?

## Pondering the Principles

1. God's Word gives us a glimpse of what our eternal reward will be like:

   • We will be like Christ: "We know that, when He appears, we shall be like Him, because we shall see Him just as He is" (1 John 3:2).

   • We will enjoy endless companionship with Christ: As Jesus Himself said, "I will come again, and receive you to Myself; that where I am, there you may be also" (John 14:3).

   • We will enjoy complete health: Our "perishable body . . . is raised an imperishable body; it is sown in dishonor, it is raised in glory; it is sown in weakness, it is raised in power" (1 Cor. 15:42-43).

   • We will enjoy unending happiness: God "shall wipe away every tear from their eyes; and there shall no longer be any death; there shall no longer be any mourning, or crying, or pain" (Rev. 21:4).

   • We will worship God forever: The apostle John said, "I heard, as it were, a loud voice of a great multitude in heaven, saying, 'Hallelujah! Salvation and glory and power belong to our God'" (Rev. 19:1).

   All those blessings await the believer. If you are not a believer, allow God's kindness to lead you to repentance (Rom. 2:4). If you are, prayerfully offer praise and thanksgiving to God for providing such eternal glory.

2. Paul's anticipation of his eternal reward affected his conduct in this life. Look up the following verses to see how you should be living in light of eternity:

- Philippians 2:14-16

- Colossians 3:2-5, 8-9, 12-17

- 1 Thessalonians 5:6-8, 11

- 2 Thessalonians 2:14-15

- 2 Peter 3:11, 14

- 1 John 3:2-3

# Scripture Index

# Topical Index

Abortion, church advocacy of, 38

Alleine, Joseph, his compulsion to preach, 47

Barclay, William
on the Battle of Marathon, 72
on literary pictures of death, 63-64
on Paul's passing the baton, 58

Baseball focus. See Williams, Ted

Baxter, Richard, on dying thoughts, 66

Bible, the. See Scripture

Big Ben, illustration of the watch that envied, 35, 41

Blind girl who loved Scripture, 73-74

Browning, his "Incident of the French Camp," 64

Bunyan, John, on the preacher's portrait, 8-9

Calf-makers, ministerial, 39

Calling
every believers', 44-45
to the ministry, 44-50

Courage, prayer and, 70

Crown, believers'. See Rewards

Death
with digniy, 64-66
final words approaching, 57-58
literary pictures of, 63-64
See also Funeral

Dignity, dying with. See Death

Earnestness, importance of, 26

Eldership. See Leadership, church

Encouragement, 27-28

Evangelism. See Preaching

Evangelist. See Preacher

Excellence, spiritual, 33-35, 41

Exhortation, 27-28

False teachers, within the professing church, 38

Feminism, church advocacy of, 38

French blind girl. See Blind girl

Funeral
African, 63
preaching at a, 27
See also Death

God, presence of, 12, 20

Hendricksen, William, on Paul's spiritual struggle, 69

Homosexuality, church advocacy of, 38

Hort, Fenton, on "sober," 40

"If--." See Kipling, Rudyard

"Incident of the French Camp." See Browning, Robert

Intolerance, of truth, 36-40

Jesus Christ, judgment by, 11-16

"Jesus, I My Cross Have Taken." See Lyte, Henry

Johnston, Jon, on spiritual excellence, 33-35

Judgment
coming, 11-16
by Jesus Christ, 11
stages of, 14
timing of, 14-16

Judgment Seat of Christ. See Rewards, believers'

Kipling, Rudyard, his poem "If--," 71-72

Knox, John
evangelistic prayer of, 10
his reluctance to preach, 10

Leadership, church
importance of understanding biblical, 17. See also Preacher

Life
meaning of, 57-58
purpose of, 33

Lloyd-Jones, Martyn
on being willing to minister, 55
on manipulative preaching, 52-53
on triumphing spiritually, 74-75

Lyte, Henry, his hymn "Jesus, I My Cross Have Taken," 66

MacArthur, John
his father's charging him to preach the Word, 20
his grandfather's eagerness to preach, 54
his track coach's challenge, 73

Man of God. See Preacher

Manipulation, sin of, 52-53

Marathon, Battle of, 72

Minister. See Preacher

Moses, steadfastness of, 42

Napoleon, as depicted in Browning's "Incident of the French Camp," 64

Neff, David, on success vs. excellence, 34

Newton, John, on the call to ministry, 49

Nobility of serving Christ, 69-70, 75

Non-Christians. See unbelievers

Pastor. See Preacher

Patience, the grace of, 28

Paul
death of, 62
epitaph of, 57-88
heavenly reward of, 80-86
triumphant epitaph of, 57-88

Pilgrim's Progress. See Bunyan, John

Pocket watch, illustration of the envious, 35, 41

Preacher
call of the, 44-50
earnestness of the, 26
evaluating the, 13, 36
judgment of the, 11-16
layman and the, 28-29